CLEP-4

COLLEGE LEVEL EXAMINATION
PROGRAM SERIES

THIS IS YOUR **PASSBOOK®** FOR ...

ANALYSIS & INTERPRETATION OF LITERATURE

NLC®

NATIONAL LEARNING CORPORATION®
passbooks.com

COPYRIGHT NOTICE

This book is SOLELY intended for, is sold ONLY to, and its use is RESTRICTED to individual, bona fide applicants or candidates who qualify by virtue of having seriously filed applications for appropriate license, certificate, professional and/or promotional advancement, higher school matriculation, scholarship, or other legitimate requirements of educational and/or governmental authorities.

This book is NOT intended for use, class instruction, tutoring, training, duplication, copying, reprinting, excerption, or adaptation, etc., by:

1) Other publishers
2) Proprietors and/or Instructors of «Coaching» and/or Preparatory Courses
3) Personnel and/or Training Divisions of commercial, industrial, and governmental organizations
4) Schools, colleges, or universities and/or their departments and staffs, including teachers and other personnel
5) Testing Agencies or Bureaus
6) Study groups which seek by the purchase of a single volume to copy and/or duplicate and/or adapt this material for use by the group as a whole without having purchased individual volumes for each of the members of the group
7) Et al.

Such persons would be in violation of appropriate Federal and State statutes.

PROVISION OF LICENSING AGREEMENTS. — Recognized educational, commercial, industrial, and governmental institutions and organizations, and others legitimately engaged in educational pursuits, including training, testing, and measurement activities, may address request for a licensing agreement to the copyright owners, who will determine whether, and under what conditions, including fees and charges, the materials in this book may be used them. In other words, a licensing facility exists for the legitimate use of the material in this book on other than an individual basis. However, it is asseverated and affirmed here that the material in this book CANNOT be used without the receipt of the express permission of such a licensing agreement from the Publishers. Inquiries re licensing should be addressed to the company, attention rights and permissions department.

All rights reserved, including the right of reproduction in whole or in part, in any form or by any means, electronic or mechanical, including photocopying, recording, or by any information storage and retrieval system, without permission in writing from the Publisher.

Copyright © 2020 by

NLC®

National Learning Corporation

212 Michael Drive, Syosset, NY 11791
(516) 921-8888 • www.passbooks.com
E-mail: info@passbooks.com

PUBLISHED IN THE UNITED STATES OF AMERICA

PASSBOOK® SERIES

THE *PASSBOOK® SERIES* has been created to prepare applicants and candidates for the ultimate academic battlefield – the examination room.

At some time in our lives, each and every one of us may be required to take an examination – for validation, matriculation, admission, qualification, registration, certification, or licensure.

Based on the assumption that every applicant or candidate has met the basic formal educational standards, has taken the required number of courses, and read the necessary texts, the *PASSBOOK® SERIES* furnishes the one special preparation which may assure passing with confidence, instead of failing with insecurity. Examination questions – together with answers – are furnished as the basic vehicle for study so that the mysteries of the examination and its compounding difficulties may be eliminated or diminished by a sure method.

This book is meant to help you pass your examination provided that you qualify and are serious in your objective.

The entire field is reviewed through the huge store of content information which is succinctly presented through a provocative and challenging approach – the question-and-answer method.

A climate of success is established by furnishing the correct answers at the end of each test.

You soon learn to recognize types of questions, forms of questions, and patterns of questioning. You may even begin to anticipate expected outcomes.

You perceive that many questions are repeated or adapted so that you can gain acute insights, which may enable you to score many sure points.

You learn how to confront new questions, or types of questions, and to attack them confidently and work out the correct answers.

You note objectives and emphases, and recognize pitfalls and dangers, so that you may make positive educational adjustments.

Moreover, you are kept fully informed in relation to new concepts, methods, practices, and directions in the field.

You discover that you arre actually taking the examination all the time: you are preparing for the examination by "taking" an examination, not by reading extraneous and/or supererogatory textbooks.

In short, this PASSBOOK®, used directedly, should be an important factor in helping you to pass your test.

NONTRADITIONAL EDUCATION

Students returning to school as adults bring more varied experience to their studies than do the teenagers who begin college shortly after graduating from high school. As a result, there are numerous programs for students with nontraditional learning curves. Hundreds of colleges and universities grant degrees to people who cannot attend classes at a regular campus or have already learned what the college is supposed to teach.

You can earn nontraditional education credits in many ways:
- Passing standardized exams
- Demonstrating knowledge gained through experience
- Completing campus-based coursework, and
- Taking courses off campus

Some methods of assessing learning for credit are objective, such as standardized tests. Others are more subjective, such as a review of life experiences.

With some help from four hypothetical characters – Alice, Vin, Lynette, and Jorge – this article describes nontraditional ways of earning educational credit. It begins by describing programs in which you can earn a high school diploma without spending 4 years in a classroom. The college picture is more complicated, so it is presented in two parts: one on gaining credit for what you know through course work or experience, and a second on college degree programs. The final section lists resources for locating more information.

Earning High School Credit

People who were prevented from finishing high school as teenagers have several options if they want to do so as adults. Some major cities have back-to-school programs that allow adults to attend high school classes with current students. But the more practical alternatives for most adults are to take the General Educational Development (GED) tests or to earn a high school diploma by demonstrating their skills or taking correspondence classes.

Of course, these options do not match the experience of staying in high school and graduating with one's friends. But they are viable alternatives for adult learners committed to meeting and, often, continuing their educational goals.

GED Program

Alice quit high school her sophomore year and took a job to help support herself, her younger brother, and their newly widowed mother. Now an adult, she wants to earn her high school diploma – and then go on to college. Because her job as head cook and her family responsibilities keep her busy during the day, she plans to get a high school equivalency diploma. She will study for, and take, the GED tests. Every year, about half a million adults earn their high school credentials this way. A GED diploma is accepted in lieu of a high school one by more than 90 percent of employers, colleges, and universities, so it is a good choice for someone like Alice.

The GED testing program is sponsored by the American Council on Education and State and local education departments. It consists of examinations in five subject areas: Writing, science, mathematics, social studies, and literature and the arts. The tests also measure skills such as analytical ability, problem solving, reading comprehension, and ability to understand and apply information. Most of the questions are multiple choice; the writing test includes an essay section on a topic of general interest.

Eligibility rules for taking the exams vary, but some states require that you must be at least 18. Tests are given in English, Spanish, and French. In addition to standard print, versions in large print, Braille, and audiocassette are also available. Total time allotted for the tests is 7 1/2 hours.

The GED tests are not easy. About one-fourth of those who complete the exams every year do not pass. Passing scores are established by administering the tests to a sample of graduating high school seniors. The minimum standard score is set so that about one-third of graduating seniors would not pass the tests if they took them.

Because of the difficulty of the tests, people need to prepare themselves to take them. Often, they start by taking the Official GED Practice Tests, usually available through a local adult education center. Centers are listed in your phone book's blue pages under "Adult Education," "Continuing Education," or "GED." Adult education centers also have information about GED preparation classes and self-study materials. Classes are generally arranged to accommodate adults' work schedules. National Learning Corporation publishes several study guides that aim to thoroughly prepare test-takers for the GED.

School districts, colleges, adult education centers, and community organizations have information about GED testing schedules and practice tests. For more information, contact them, your nearest GED testing center, or:

GED Testing Service
One Dupont Circle, NW, Suite 250
Washington, DC 20036-1163
1(800) 62-MY GED (626-9433)
(202) 939-9490

Skills Demonstration

Adults who have acquired high school level skills through experience might be eligible for the National External Diploma Program. This alternative to the GED does not involve any direct instruction. Instead, adults seeking a high school diploma must demonstrate mastery of 65 competencies in 8 general areas: Communication; computation; occupational preparedness; and self, social, consumer, scientific, and technological awareness.

Mastery is shown through the completion of the tasks. For example, a participant could prove competency in computation by measuring a room for carpeting, figuring out the amount of carpet needed, and computing the cost.

Before being accepted for the program, adults undergo an evaluation. Tests taken at one of the program's offices measure reading, writing, and mathematics abilities. A take-home segment includes a self-assessment of current skills, an individual skill evaluation, and an occupational interest and aptitude test.

Adults accepted for the program have weekly meetings with an assessor. At the meeting, the assessor reviews the participant's work from the previous week. If the task has not been completed properly, the assessor explains the mistake. Participants continue to correct their errors until they master each competency. A high school diploma is awarded upon proven mastery of all 65 competencies.

Fourteen States and the District of Columbia now offer the External Diploma Program. For more information, contact:

External Diploma Program
One Dupont Circle, NW, Suite 250
Washington, DC 20036-1193
(202) 939-9475

Correspondence and Distance Study

Vin dropped out of high school during his junior year because his family's frequent moves made it difficult for him to continue his studies. He promised himself at the time he dropped out that he would someday finish the courses needed for his diploma. For people like Vin, who prefer to earn a traditional diploma in a nontraditional way, there are about a dozen accredited courses of study for earning a high school diploma by correspondence, or distance study. The programs are either privately run, affiliated with a university, or administered by a State education department.

Distance study diploma programs have no residency requirements, allowing students to continue their studies from almost any location. Depending on the course of study, students need not be enrolled full time and usually have more flexible schedules for finishing their work. Selection of courses ranges from vo-tech to college prep, and some programs place different emphasis on the types of diplomas offered. University affiliated schools, for example, allow qualified students to take college courses along with their high school ones. Students can then apply the college credits toward a degree at that university or transfer them to another institution.

Taking courses by distance study is often more challenging and time consuming than attending classes, especially for adults who have other obligations. Success depends on each student's motivation. Students usually do reading assignments on their own. Written exercises, which they complete and send to an instructor for grading, supplement their reading material.

A list of some accredited high schools that offer diplomas by distance study is available free from the Distance Education and Training Council, formerly known as the National Home Study Council. Request the "DETC Directory of Accredited Institutions" from:

The Distance Education and Training Council
1601 18th Street, NW.
Washington, DC 20009-2529
(202) 234-5100

Some publications profiling nontraditional college programs include addresses and descriptions of several high school correspondence ones. See the Resources section at the end of this article for more information.

Getting College Credit For What You Know

Adults can receive college credit for prior coursework, by passing examinations, and documenting experiential learning. With help from a college advisor, nontraditional students should assess their skills, establish their educational goals, and determine the number of college credits they might be eligible for.

Even before you meet with a college advisor, you should collect all your school and training records. Then, make a list of all knowledge and abilities acquired through experience, no matter how irrelevant they seem to your chosen field. Next, determine your educational goals: What specific field do you wish to study? What kind of a degree do you want? Finally, determine how your past work fits into the field of study. Later on, you will evaluate educational programs to find one that's right for you.

People who have complex educational or experiential learning histories might want to have their learning evaluated by the Regents Credit Bank. The Credit Bank, operated by Regents College of the University of the State of New York, allows people to consolidate credits earned through college, experience, or other methods. Special assessments are available for Regents College enrollees whose knowledge in a specific field cannot be adequately evaluated by standardized exams. For more information, contact the Regents Credit Bank at:

Regents College
7 Columbia Circle
Albany, NY 12203-5159
(518) 464-8500

Credit For Prior College Coursework

When Lynette was in college during the 1970s, she attended several different schools and took a variety of courses. She did well in some classes and poorly in others. Now that she is a successful business owner and has more focus, Lynette thinks she should forget about her previous coursework and start from scratch. Instead, she should start from where she is.

Lynette should have all her transcripts sent to the colleges or universities of her choice and let an admissions officer determine which classes are applicable toward a degree. A few credits here and there may not seem like much, but they add up. Even if the subjects do not seem relevant to any major, they might be counted as elective credits toward a degree. And comparing the cost of transcripts with the cost of college courses, it makes sense to spend a few dollars per transcript for a chance to save hundreds, and perhaps thousands, of dollars in books and tuition.

Rules for transferring credits apply to all prior coursework at accredited colleges and universities, whether done on campus or off. Courses completed off campus, often called extended learning, include those available to students through independent study and correspondence. Many schools have extended learning programs; Brigham Young University, for example, offers more than 300 courses through its Department of Independent Study. One type of extended learning is distance learning, a form of correspondence study by technological means such as television, video and audio, CD-ROM, electronic mail, and computer tutorials. See the Resources section at the end of this article for more information about publications available from the National University Continuing Education Association.

Any previously earned college credits should be considered for transfer, no matter what the subject or the grade received. Many schools do not accept the transfer of courses graded below a C or ones taken more than a designated number of years ago. Some colleges and universities also have limits on the number of credits that can be transferred and applied toward a degree. But not all do. For example, Thomas Edison State College, New Jersey's State college for adults, accepts the transfer of all 120 hours of credit required for a baccalaureate degree – provided all the credits are transferred from regionally accredited schools, no more than 80 are at the junior college level, and the student's grades overall and in the field of study average out to C.

To assign credit for prior coursework, most schools require original transcripts. This means you must complete a form or send a written, signed request to have your transcripts released directly to a college or university. Once you have chosen the schools you want to apply to, contact the schools you attended before. Find out how much each transcript costs, and ask them to send your transcripts to the ones you are applying to. Write a letter that includes your name (and names used during attendance, if different) and dates of attendance, along with the names and addresses of the schools to which your transcripts should be sent. Include payment and mail to the registrar at the schools you have attended. The registrar's office will process your request and send an official transcript of your coursework to the colleges or universities you have designated.

Credit For Noncollege Courses

Colleges and universities are not the only ones that offer classes. Volunteer organizations and employers often provide formal training worth college credit. The American Council on Education has two programs that assess thousands of specific courses and make recommendations on the amount of college credit they are worth. Colleges and universities accept the recommendations or use them as guidelines.

One program evaluates educational courses sponsored by government agencies, business and industry, labor unions, and professional and voluntary organizations. It is the Program on Noncollegiate Sponsored Instruction (PONSI). Some of the training seminars Alice has participated in covered topics such as food preparation, kitchen safety, and nutrition. Although she has not yet earned her GED, Alice can earn college credit because of her completion of these formal job-training seminars. The number of credits each seminar is worth does not hinge on Alice's current eligibility for college enrollment.

The other program evaluates courses offered by the Army, Navy, Air Force, Marines, Coast Guard, and Department of Defense. It is the Military Evaluations Program. Jorge has never attended college, but the engineering technology classes he completed as part of his military training are worth college credit. And as an Army veteran, Jorge is eligible for a service that takes the evaluations one step further. The Army/American Council on Education Registry Transcript System (AARTS) will provide Jorge with an individualized transcript of American Council on Education credit recommendations for all courses he completed, the military occupational specialties (MOS's) he held, and examinations he passed while in the Army. All Army and National Guard enlisted personnel and veterans who enlisted after October 1981 are eligible for the transcript. Similar services are being considered by the Navy and Marine Corps.

To obtain a free transcript, see your Army Education Center for a 5454R transcript request form. Include your name, Social Security number, basic active service date, and complete address where you want the transcript sent. Mail your request to:
AARTS Operations Center
415 McPherson Ave.
Fort Leavenworth, KS 66027-1373

Recommendations for PONSI are published in *The National Guide to Educational Credit for Training Programs;* military program recommendations are in *The Guide to the Evaluation of Educational Experiences in the Armed Forces.* See the Resources section at the end of this article for more information about these publications.

Former military personnel who took a foreign language course through the Defense Language Institute may request course transcripts by sending their name, Social Security number, course title, duration of the course, and graduation date to:

> Commandant, Defense Language Institute
> Attn: ATFL-DAA-AR
> Transcripts
> Presidio of Monterey
> Monterey, CA 93944-5006

Not all of Jorge's and Alice's courses have been assessed by the American Council on Education. Training courses that have no Council credit recommendation should still be assessed by an advisor at the schools they want to attend. Course descriptions, class notes, test scores, and other documentation may be helpful for comparing training courses to their college equivalents. An oral examination or other demonstration of competency might also be required.

There is no guarantee you will receive all the credits you are seeking – but you certainly won't if you make no attempt.

Credit By Examination

Standardized tests are the best-known method of receiving college credit without taking courses. These exams are often taken by high school students seeking advanced placement for college, but they are also available to adult learners. Testing programs and colleges and universities offer exams in a number of subjects. Two U.S. Government institutes have foreign language exams for employees that also may be worth college credit.

It is important to understand that receiving a passing score on these exams does not mean you get college credit automatically. Each school determines which test results it will accept, minimum scores required, how scores are converted for credit, and the amount of credit, if any, to be assigned. Most colleges and universities accept the American Council on Education credit recommendations, published every other year in the 250-page *Guide to Educational Credit by Examination*. For more information, contact:

> The American Council on Education
> Credit by Examination Program
> One Dupont Circle, Suite 250
> Washington, DC 20036-1193
> (202) 939-9434

Testing programs:

You might know some of the five national testing programs by their acronyms or initials: CLEP, ACT PEP: RCE, DANTES, AP, and NOCTI. (The meanings of these initialisms are explained below.) There is some overlap among programs; for example, four of them have introductory accounting exams. Since you will not be awarded credit more than once for a specific subject, you should carefully evaluate each program for the subject exams you wish to take. And before taking an exam, make sure you will be awarded credit by the college or university you plan to attend.

CLEP (College-Level Examination Program), administered by the College Board, is the most widely accepted of the national testing programs; more than 2,800 accredited schools award credit for passing exam scores. Each test covers material taught in basic undergraduate courses. There are five general exams – English composition, humanities, college mathematics, natural sciences, and social sciences and history – and many subject exams. Most exams are entirely multiple-choice, but English composition exams may include an essay section. For more information, contact:

    CLEP
    P.O. Box 6600
    Princeton, NJ 08541-6600
    (609) 771-7865

ACT PEP: RCE (American College Testing Proficiency Exam Program: Regents College Examinations) tests are given in 38 subjects within arts and sciences, business, education, and nursing. Each exam is recommended for either lower- or upper-level credit. Exams contain either objective or extended response questions, and are graded according to a standard score, letter grade, or pass/fail. Fees vary, depending on the subject and type of exam. For more information or to request free study guides, contact:

    ACT PEP: Regents College Examinations
    P.O. Box 4014
    Iowa City, IA 52243
    (319) 337-1387
    (New York State residents must contact Regents College directly.)

DANTES (Defense Activity for Nontraditional Education Support) standardized tests are developed by the Educational Testing Service for the Department of Defense. Originally administered only to military personnel, the exams have been available to the public since 1983. About 50 subject tests cover business, mathematics, social science, physical science, humanities, foreign languages, and applied technology. Most of the tests consist entirely of multiple-choice questions. Schools determine their own administering fees and testing schedules. For more information or to request free study sheets, contact:

    DANTES Program Office
    Mail Stop 31-X
    Educational Testing Service
    Princeton, NJ 08541
    1(800) 257-9484

The AP (Advanced Placement) Program is a cooperative effort between secondary schools and colleges and universities. AP exams are developed each year by committees of college and high school faculty appointed by the College Board and assisted by consultants from the Educational Testing Service. Subjects include arts and languages, natural sciences, computer science, social sciences, history, and mathematics. Most tests are 2 or 3 hours long and include both multiple-choice and essay questions. AP courses are available to help students prepare for exams, which are offered in the spring. For more information about the Advanced Placement Program, contact:

    Advanced Placement Services
    P.O. Box 6671
    Princeton, NJ 08541-6671
    (609) 771-7300

NOCTI (National Occupational Competency Testing Institute) assessments are designed for people like Alice, who have vocational-technical skills that cannot be evaluated by other tests. NOCTI assesses competency at two levels: Student/job ready and teacher/experienced worker. Standardized evaluations are available for occupations such as auto-body repair, electronics, mechanical drafting, quantity food preparation, and upholstering. The tests consist of multiple-choice questions and a performance component. Other services include workshops, customized assessments, and pre-testing. For more information, contact:

NOCTI
500 N. Bronson Ave.
Ferris State University
Big Rapids, MI 49307
(616) 796-4699

Colleges and universities:

Many colleges and universities have credit-by-exam programs, through which students earn credit by passing a comprehensive exam for a course offered by the institution. Among the most widely recognized are the programs at Ohio University, the University of North Carolina, Thomas Edison State College, and New York University.

Ohio University offers about 150 examinations for credit. In addition, you may sometimes arrange to take special examinations in non-laboratory courses offered at Ohio University. To take a test for credit, you must enroll in the course. If you plan to transfer the credit earned, you also need written permission from an official at your school. Books and study materials are available, for a cost, through the university. Exams must be taken within 6 months of the enrollment date; most last 3 hours. You may arrange to take the exam off campus if you do not live near the university.

Ohio University is on the quarter-hour system; most courses are worth 4 quarter hours, the equivalent of 3 semester hours. For more information, contact:

Independent Study
Tupper Hall 302
Ohio University
Athens, OH 45701-2979
1(800) 444-2910
(614) 593-2910

The University of North Carolina offers a credit-by-examination option for 140 independent study (correspondence) courses in foreign languages, humanities, social sciences, mathematics, business administration, education, electrical and computer engineering, health administration, and natural sciences. To take an exam, you must request and receive approval from both the course instructor and the independent studies department. Exams must be taken within six months of enrollment, and you may register for no more than two at a time. If you are not near the University's Chapel Hill campus, you may take your exam under supervision at an accredited college, university, community college, or technical institute. For more information, contact:

Independent Studies
CB #1020, The Friday Center
UNC-Chapel Hill
Chapel Hill, NC 27599-1020
1(800) 862-5669 / (919) 962-1134

The Thomas Edison College Examination Program offers more than 50 exams in liberal arts, business, and professional areas. Thomas Edison State College administers tests twice a month in Trenton, New Jersey; however, students may arrange to take their tests with a proctor at any accredited American college or university or U.S. military base. Most of the tests are multiple choice; some also include short answer or essay questions. Time limits range from 90 minutes to 4 hours, depending on the exam. For more information, contact:

Thomas Edison State College
TECEP, Office of Testing and Assessment
101 W. State Street
Trenton, NJ 08608-1176
(609) 633-2844

New York University's Foreign Language Program offers proficiency exams in more than 40 languages, from Albanian to Yiddish. Two exams are available in each language: The 12-point test is equivalent to 4 undergraduate semesters, and the 16-point exam may lead to upper level credit. The tests are given at the university's Foreign Language Department throughout the year.

Proof of foreign language proficiency does not guarantee college credit. Some colleges and universities accept transcripts only for languages commonly taught, such as French and Spanish. Nontraditional programs are more likely than traditional ones to grant credit for proficiency in other languages.

For an informational brochure and registration form for NYU's foreign language proficiency exams, contact:

New York University
Foreign Language Department
48 Cooper Square, Room 107
New York, NY 10003
(212) 998-7030

Government institutes:

The Defense Language Institute and Foreign Service Institute administer foreign language proficiency exams for personnel stationed abroad. Usually, the tests are given at the end of intensive language courses or upon completion of service overseas. But some people – like Jorge, who knows Spanish – speak another language fluently and may be allowed to take a proficiency exam in that language before completing their tour of duty. Contact one of the offices listed below to obtain transcripts of those scores. Proof of proficiency does not guarantee college credit, however, as discussed above.

To request score reports from the Defense Language Institute for Defense Language Proficiency Tests, send your name, Social Security number, language for which you were tested, and, most importantly, when and where you took the exam to:

Commandant, Defense Language Institute
Attn: ATFL-ES-T
DLPT Score Report Request
Presidio of Monterey
Monterey, CA 93944-5006

To request transcripts of scores for Foreign Service Institute exams, send your name, Social Security number, language for which you were tested, and dates or year of exams to:

Foreign Service Institute
Arlington Hall
4020 Arlington Boulevard
Rosslyn, VA 22204-1500
Attn: Testing Office (Send your request to the attention of the testing office of the foreign language in which you were tested)

Credit For Experience

Experiential learning credit may be given for knowledge gained through job responsibilities, personal hobbies, volunteer opportunities, homemaking, and other experiences. Colleges and universities base credit awards on the knowledge you have attained, not for the experience alone. In addition, the knowledge must be college level; not just any learning will do. Throwing horseshoes as a hobby is not likely to be worth college credit. But if you've done research on how and where the sport originated, visited blacksmiths, organized tournaments, and written a column for a trade journal – well, that's a horseshoe of a different color.

Adults attempting to get credit for their experience should be forewarned: Having your experience evaluated for college credit is time-consuming, tedious work – not an easy shortcut for people who want quick-fix college credits. And not all experience, no matter how valuable, is the equivalent of college courses.

Requesting college credit for your experiential learning can be tricky. You should get assistance from a credit evaluations officer at the school you plan to attend, but you should also have a general idea of what your knowledge is worth. A common method for converting knowledge into credit is to use a college catalog. Find course titles and descriptions that match what you have learned through experience, and request the number of credits offered for those courses.

Once you know what credit to ask for, you must usually present your case in writing to officials at the college you plan to attend. The most common form of presenting experiential learning for credit is the portfolio. A portfolio is a written record of your knowledge along with a request for equivalent college credit. It includes an identification and description of the knowledge for which you are requesting credit, an explanatory essay of how the knowledge was gained and how it fits into your educational plans, documentation that you have acquired such knowledge, and a request for college credit. Required elements of a portfolio vary by schools but generally follow those guidelines.

In identifying knowledge you have gained, be specific about exactly what you have learned. For example, it is not enough for Lynette to say she runs a business. She must identify the knowledge she has gained from running it, such as personnel management, tax law, marketing strategy, and inventory review. She must also include brief descriptions about her knowledge of each to support her claims of having those skills.

The essay gives you a chance to relay something about who you are. It should address your educational goals, include relevant autobiographical details, and be well organized, neat, and convey confidence. In his essay, Jorge might first state his goal of becoming an engineer. Then he would explain why he joined the Army, where he got hands-on training and experience in developing and servicing electronic equipment.

This, he would say, led to his hobby of creating remote-controlled model cars, of which he has built 20. His conclusion would highlight his accomplishments and tie them to his desire to become an electronic engineer.

Documentation is evidence that you've learned what you claim to have learned. You can show proof of knowledge in a variety of ways, including audio or video recordings, letters from current or former employers describing your specific duties and job performance, blueprints, photographs or artwork, and transcripts of certifying exams for professional licenses and certification – such as Alice's certification from the American Culinary Federation. Although documentation can take many forms, written proof alone is not always enough. If it is impossible to document your knowledge in writing, find out if your experiential learning can be assessed through supplemental oral exams by a faculty expert.

Earning a College Degree

Nontraditional students often have work, family, and financial obligations that prevent them from quitting their jobs to attend school full time. Can they still meet their educational goals? Yes.

More than 150 accredited colleges and universities have nontraditional bachelor's degree programs that require students to spend little or no time on campus; over 300 others have nontraditional campus-based degree programs. Some of those schools, as well as most junior and community colleges, offer associate's degrees nontraditionally. Each school with a nontraditional course of study determines its own rules for awarding credit for prior coursework, exams, or experience, as discussed previously. Most have charges on top of tuition for providing these special services.

Several publications profile nontraditional degree programs; see the Resources section at the end of this article for more information. To determine which school best fits your academic profile and educational goals, first list your criteria. Then, evaluate nontraditional programs based on their accreditation, features, residency requirements, and expenses. Once you have chosen several schools to explore further, write to them for more information. Detailed explanations of school policies should help you decide which ones you want to apply to.

Get beyond the printed word – especially the glowing words each school writes about itself. Check out the schools you are considering with higher education authorities, alumni, employers, family members, and friends. If possible, visit the campus to talk to students and instructors and sit in on a few classes, even if you will be completing most or all of your work off campus. Ask school officials questions about such things as enrollment numbers, graduation rate, faculty qualifications, and confusing details about the application process or academic policies. After you have thoroughly investigated each prospective college or university, you can make an informed decision about which is right for you.

Accreditation

Accreditation is a process colleges and universities submit to voluntarily for getting their credentials. An accredited school has been investigated and visited by teams of observers and has periodic inspections by a private accrediting agency. The initial review can take two years or more.

Regional agencies accredit entire schools, and professional agencies accredit either specialized schools or departments within schools. Although there are no national accrediting standards, not just any accreditation will do. Countless "accreditation associations" have been invented by schools, many of which have no academic programs and sell phony degrees, to accredit themselves. But 6 regional and about 80 professional accrediting associations in the United States are recognized by the U.S. Department of Education or the Commission on Recognition of Postsecondary Accreditation. When checking accreditation, these are the names to look for. For more information about accreditation and accrediting agencies, contact:

> Institutional Participation Oversight Service Accreditation and State Liaison Division
> U.S. Department of Education
> ROB 3, Room 3915
> 600 Independence Ave., SW
> Washington, DC 20202-5244
> (202) 708-7417

Because accreditation is not mandatory, lack of accreditation does not necessarily mean a school or program is bad. Some schools choose not to apply for accreditation, are in the process of applying, or have educational methods too unconventional for an accrediting association's standards. For the nontraditional student, however, earning a degree from a college or university with recognized accreditation is an especially important consideration. Although nontraditional education is becoming more widely accepted, it is not yet mainstream. Employers skeptical of a degree earned in a nontraditional manner are likely to be even less accepting of one from an unaccredited school.

Program Features

Because nontraditional students have diverse educational objectives, nontraditional schools are diverse in what they offer. Some programs are geared toward helping students organize their scattered educational credits to get a degree as quickly as possible. Others cater to those who may have specific credits or experience but need assistance in completing requirements. Whatever your educational profile, you should look for a program that works with you in obtaining your educational goals.

A few nontraditional programs have special admissions policies for adult learners like Alice, who plan to earn their GEDs but want to enroll in college in the meantime. Other features of nontraditional programs include individualized learning agreements, intensive academic counseling, cooperative learning and internship placement, and waiver of some prerequisites or other requirements – as well as college credit for prior coursework, examinations, and experiential learning, all discussed previously.

Lynette, whose primary goal is to finish her degree, wants to earn maximum credits for her business experience. She will look for programs that do not limit the number of credits awarded for equivalency exams and experiential learning. And since well-documented proof of knowledge is essential for earning experiential learning credits, Lynette should make sure the program she chooses provides assistance to students submitting a portfolio.

Jorge, on the other hand, has more credits than he needs in certain areas and is willing to forego some. To become an engineer, he must have a bachelor's degree; but because he is accustomed to hands-on learning, Jorge is interested in getting experience as he gains more technical skills. He will concentrate on finding schools with strong cooperative education, supervised fieldwork, or internship programs.

Residency Requirements

Programs are sometimes deemed nontraditional because of their residency requirements. Many people think of residency for colleges and universities in terms of tuition, with in-state students paying less than out-of-state ones. Residency also may refer to where a student lives, either on or off campus, while attending school.

But in nontraditional education, residency usually refers to how much time students must spend on campus, regardless of whether they attend classes there. In some nontraditional programs, students need not ever step foot on campus. Others require only a very short residency, such as one day or a few weeks. Many schools have standard residency requirements of several semesters but schedule classes for evenings or weekends to accommodate working adults.

Lynette, who previously took courses by independent study, prefers to earn credits by distance study. She will focus on schools that have no residency requirement. Several colleges and universities have nonresident degree completion programs for adults with some college credit. Under the direction of a faculty advisor, students devise a plan for earning their remaining credits. Methods for earning credits include independent study, distance learning, seminars, supervised fieldwork, and group study at arranged sites. Students may have to earn a certain number of credits through the degree-granting institution. But many programs allow students to take courses at accredited schools of their choice for transfer toward their degree.

Alice wants to attend lectures but has an unpredictable schedule. Her best course of action will be to seek out short residency programs that require students to attend seminars once or twice a semester. She can take courses that are televised and videotape them to watch when her schedule permits, with the seminars helping to ensure that she properly completes her coursework. Many colleges and universities with short residency requirements also permit students to earn some credits elsewhere, by whatever means the student chooses.

Some fields of study require classroom instruction. As Jorge will discover, few colleges and universities allow students to earn a bachelor's degree in engineering entirely through independent study. Nontraditional residency programs are designed to accommodate adults' daytime work schedules. Jorge should look for programs offering evening, weekend, summer, and accelerated courses.

Tuition and Other Expenses

The final decisions about which schools Alice, Jorge, and Lynette attend may hinge in large part on a single issue: Cost. And rising tuition is only part of the equation. Beginning with application fees and continuing through graduation fees, college expenses add up.

Traditional and nontraditional students have some expenses in common, such as the cost of books and other materials. Tuition might even be the same for some courses, especially for colleges and universities offering standard ones at unusual times. But for nontraditional programs, students may also pay fees for services such as credit or transcript review, evaluation, advisement, and portfolio assessment.

Students are also responsible for postage and handling or setup expenses for independent study courses, as well as for all examination and transcript fees for transferring credits. Usually, the more nontraditional the program, the more detailed the fees. Some schools charge a yearly enrollment fee rather than tuition for degree completion candidates who want their files to remain active.

Although tuition and fees might seem expensive, most educators tell you not to let money come between you and your educational goals. Talk to someone in the financial aid department of the school you plan to attend or check your library for publications about financial aid sources. The U.S. Department of Education publishes a guide to Federal aid programs such as Pell Grants, student loans, and work-study. To order the free 74-page booklet, *The Student Guide: Financial Aid from the U.S. Department of Education,* contact:

> Federal Student Aid Information Center
> P.O. Box 84
> Washington, DC 20044
> 1 (800) 4FED-AID (433-3243)

Resources

Information on how to earn a high school diploma or college degree without following the usual routes is available from several organizations and in numerous publications. Information on nontraditional graduate degree programs, available for master's through doctoral level, though not discussed in this article, can usually be obtained from the same resources that detail bachelor's degree programs.

National Learning Corporation publishes study guides for all of these exams, for both general examinations and tests in specific subject areas. To order study guides, or to browse their catalog featuring more than 5,000 titles, visit NLC online at www.passbooks.com, or contact them by phone at (800) 632-8888.

Organizations

Adult learners should always contact their local school system, community college, or university to learn about programs that are readily available. The following national organizations can also supply information:

> American Council on Education
> One Dupont Circle
> Washington, DC 20036-1193
> (202) 939-9300

Within the American Council on Education, the Center for Adult Learning and Educational Credentials administers the National External Diploma Program, the GED Program, the Program on Noncollegiate Sponsored Instruction, the Credit by Examination Program, and the Military Evaluations Program.

College-Level Examination Program (CLEP)

1. WHAT IS CLEP?

CLEP stands for the College-Level Examination Program, sponsored by the College Board. It is a national program of credit-by-examination that offers you the opportunity to obtain recognition for college-level achievement. No matter when, where, or how you have learned – by means of formal or informal study – you can take CLEP tests. If the results are acceptable to your college, you can receive credit.

You may not realize it, but you probably know more than your academic record reveals. Each day you, like most people, have an opportunity to learn. In private industry and business, as well as at all levels of government, learning opportunities continually occur. If you read widely or intensively in a particular field, think about what you read, discuss it with your family and friends, you are learning. Or you may be learning on a more formal basis by taking a correspondence course, a television or radio course, a course recorded on tape or cassettes, a course assembled into programmed tests, or a course taught in your community adult school or high school.

No matter how, where, or when you gained your knowledge, you may have the opportunity to receive academic credit for your achievement that can be counted toward an undergraduate degree. The College-Level Examination Program (CLEP) enables colleges to evaluate your achievement and give you credit. A wide range of college-level examinations are offered by CLEP to anyone who wishes to take them. Scores on the tests are reported to you and, if you wish, to a college, employer, or individual.

2. WHAT ARE THE PURPOSES OF THE COLLEGE-LEVEL EXAMINATION PROGRAM?

The basic purpose of the College-Level Examination Program is to enable individuals who have acquired their education in nontraditional ways to demonstrate their academic achievement. It is also intended for use by those in higher education, business, industry, government, and other fields who need a reliable method of assessing a person's educational level.

Recognizing that the real issue is not how a person has acquired his education but what education he has, the College Level Examination Program has been designed to serve a variety of purposes. The basic purpose, as listed above, is to enable those who have reached the college level of education in nontraditional ways to assess the level of their achievement and to use the test results in seeking college credit or placement.

In addition, scores on the tests can be used to validate educational experience obtained at a nonaccredited institution or through noncredit college courses.

Some colleges and universities may use the tests to measure the level of educational achievement of their students, and for various institutional research purposes.

Other colleges and universities may wish to use the tests in the admission, placement, and guidance of students who wish to transfer from one institution to another.

Businesses, industries, governmental agencies, and professional groups now accept the results of these tests as a basis for advancement, eligibility for further training, or professional or semi-professional certification.

Many people are interested in the examination simply to assess their own educational progress and attainment.

The college, university, business, industry, or government agency that adopts the tests in the College-Level Examination Program makes its own decision about how it will use and interpret the test scores. The College Board will provide the tests, score them, and report the results either to the individuals who took the tests or the college or agency that administered them. It does NOT, and cannot, award college credit, certify college equivalency, or make recommendations regarding the standards these institutions should establish for the use of the test results.

Therefore, if you are taking the tests to secure credit from an institution, you should FIRST ascertain whether the college or agency involved will accept the scores. Each institution determines which CLEP tests it will accept for credit and the amount of credit it will award. If you want to take tests for college credit, first call, write, or visit the college you wish to attend to inquire about its policy on CLEP scores, as well as its other admission requirements.

The services of the program are also available to people who have been requested to take the tests by an employer, a professional licensing agency, a certifying agency, or by other groups that recognize college equivalency on the basis of satisfactory CLEP scores. You may, of course, take the tests SOLELY for your own information. If you do, your scores will be reported only to you.

While neither CLEP nor the College Board can evaluate previous credentials or award college credit, you will receive, with your scores, basic information to help you interpret your performance on the tests you have taken.

3. WHAT ARE THE COLLEGE-LEVEL EXAMINATIONS?

In order to meet different kinds of curricular organization and testing needs at colleges and universities, the College-Level Examination Program offers 35 different subject tests falling under five separate general categories: Composition and Literature, Foreign Languages, History and Social Sciences, Science and Mathematics, and Business.

4. WHAT ARE THE SUBJECT EXAMINATIONS?

The 35 CLEP tests offered by the College Board are listed below:

COMPOSITION AND LITERATURE:
- American Literature
- Analyzing and Interpreting Literature
- English Composition
- English Composition with Essay
- English Literature
- Freshman College Composition
- Humanities

FOREIGN LANGUAGES
- French
- German
- Spanish

HISTORY AND SOCIAL SCIENCES
- American Government
- Introduction to Educational Psychology
- History of the United States I: Early Colonization to 1877
- History of the United States II: 1865 to the Present
- Human Growth and Development
- Principles of Macroeconomics
- Principles of Microeconomics
- Introductory Psychology
- Social Sciences and History
- Introductory Sociology
- Western Civilization I: Ancient Near East to 1648
- Western Civilization II: 1648 to the Present

SCIENCE AND MATHEMATICS
- College Algebra
- College Algebra-Trigonometry
- Biology
- Calculus
- Chemistry
- College Mathematics
- Natural Sciences
- Trigonometry
- Precalculus

BUSINESS
- Financial Accounting
- Introductory Business Law
- Information Systems and Computer Applications
- Principles of Management
- Principles of Marketing

CLEP Examinations cover material taught in courses that most students take as requirements in the first two years of college. A college usually grants the same amount of credit to students earning satisfactory scores on the CLEP examination as it grants to students successfully completing the equivalent course.

Many examinations are designed to correspond to one-semester courses; some, however, correspond to full-year or two-year courses.

Each exam is 90 minutes long and, except for English Composition with Essay, is made up primarily of multiple-choice questions. Some tests have several other types of questions besides multiple choice. To see a more detailed description of a particular CLEP exam, visit www.collegeboard.com/clep.

The English Composition with Essay exam is the only exam that includes a required essay. This essay is scored by college English faculty designated by CLEP and does not require an additional fee. However, other Composition and Literature tests offer optional essays, which some college and universities require and some do not. These essays are graded by faculty at the individual institutions that require them and require an additional $10 fee. Contact the particular institution to ask about essay requirements, and check with your test center for further details.

All 35 CLEP examinations are administered on computer. If you are unfamiliar with taking a test on a computer, consult the CLEP Sampler online at www.collegeboard.com/clep. The Sampler contains the same tutorials as the actual exams and helps familiarize you with navigation and how to answer different types of questions.

Points are not deducted for wrong or skipped answers – you receive one point for every correct answer. Therefore it is best that an answer is supplied for each exam question, whether it is a guess or not. The number of correct answers is then converted to a formula score. This formula, or "scaled," score is determined by a statistical process called *equating*, which adjusts for slight differences in difficulty between test forms and ensures that your score does not depend on the specific test form you took or how well others did on the same form. The scaled scores range from 20 to 80 – this is the number that will appear on your score report.

To ensure that you complete all questions in the time allotted, you would probably be wise to skip the more difficult or perplexing questions and return to them later. Although the multiple-choice items in these tests are carefully designed so as not to be tricky, misleading, or ambiguous, on the other hand, they are not all direct questions of factual information. They attempt, in their way, to elicit a response that indicates your knowledge or lack of knowledge of the material in question or your ability or inability to use or interpret a fact or idea. Thus, you should concentrate on answering the questions as they appear to be without attempting to out-guess the testmakers.

5. WHAT ARE THE FEES?

The fee for all CLEP examinations is $55. Optional essays required by some institutions are an additional $10.

6. WHEN ARE THE TESTS GIVEN?

CLEP tests are administered year-round. Consult the CLEP website (www.collegeboard.com/clep) and individual test centers for specific information.

7. WHERE ARE THE TESTS GIVEN?

More than 1,300 test centers are located on college and university campuses throughout the country, and additional centers are being established to meet increased needs. Any accredited collegiate institution with an explicit and publicly available policy of credit by examination can become a CLEP test center. To obtain a list of these centers, visit the CLEP website at www.collegeboard.com/clep.

8. HOW DO I REGISTER FOR THE COLLEGE-LEVEL EXAMINATION PROGRAM?

Contact an individual test center for information regarding registration, scheduling and fees. Registration/admission forms can also be obtained on the CLEP website.

9. MAY I REPEAT THE COLLEGE-LEVEL EXAMINATIONS?

You may repeat any examination providing at least six months have passed since you were last administered this test. If you repeat a test within a period of time less than six months, your scores will be cancelled and your fees forfeited. To repeat a test, check the appropriate space on the registration form.

10. WHEN MAY I EXPECT MY SCORE REPORTS?

With the exception of the English Composition with Essay exam, you should receive your score report instantly once the test is complete.

11. HOW SHOULD I PREPARE FOR THE COLLEGE-LEVEL EXAMINATIONS?

This book has been specifically designed to prepare candidates for these examinations. It will help you to consider, study, and review important content, principles, practices, procedures, problems, and techniques in the form of varied and concrete applications.

12. QUESTIONS AND ANSWERS APPEARING IN THIS PUBLICATION

The College-Level Examinations are offered by the College Board. Since copies of past examinations have not been made available, we have used equivalent materials, including questions and answers, which are highly recommended by us as an appropriate means of preparing for these examinations.

If you need additional information about CLEP Examinations, visit www.collegeboard.com/clep.

THE COLLEGE-LEVEL EXAMINATION PROGRAM

How The Program Works

CLEP examinations are administered at many colleges and universities across the country, and most institutions award college credit to those who do well on them. The examinations provide people who have acquired knowledge outside the usual educational settings the opportunity to show that they have learned college-level material without taking certain college courses.

The CLEP examinations cover material that is taught in introductory-level courses at many colleges and universities. Faculties at individual colleges review the tests to ensure that they cover the important material taught in their courses. Colleges differ in the examinations they accept; some colleges accept only two or three of the examinations while others accept nearly all of them.

Although CLEP is sponsored by the College Board and the examinations are scored by Educational Testing Service (ETS), neither of these organizations can award college credit. Only accredited colleges may grant credit toward a degree. When you take a CLEP examination, you may request that a copy of your score report be sent to the college you are attending or plan to attend. After evaluating your scores, the college will decide whether or not to award you credit for a certain course or courses, or to exempt you from them. If the college gives you credit, it will record the number of credits on your permanent record, thereby indicating that you have completed work equivalent to a course in that subject. If the college decides to grant exemption without giving you credit for a course, you will be permitted to omit a course that would normally be required of you and to take a course of your choice instead.

What the Examinations Are Like

The examinations consist mostly of multiple-choice questions to be answered within a 90-minute time limit. Additional information about each CLEP examination is given in the examination guide and on the CLEP website.

Where To Take the Examinations

CLEP examinations are administered throughout the year at the test centers of approximately 1,300 colleges and universities. On the CLEP website, you will find a list of institutions that award credit for satisfactory scores on CLEP examinations. Some colleges administer CLEP examinations to their own students only. Other institutions administer the tests to anyone who registers to take them. If your college does not administer the tests, contact the test centers in your area for information about its testing schedule.

Once you have been tested, your score report will be available instantly. CLEP scores are kept on file at ETS for 20 years; and during this period, for a small fee, you may have your transcript sent to another college or to anyone else you specify. (Your scores will never be sent to anyone without your approval.)

APPROACHING A COLLEGE ABOUT CLEP

The following sections provide a step-by-step approach to learning about the CLEP policy at a particular college or university. The person or office that can best assist students desiring CLEP credit may have a different title at each institution, but the following guidelines will lead you to information about CLEP at any institution.

Adults returning to college often benefit from special assistance when they approach a college. Opportunities for adults to return to formal learning in the classroom are now widespread, and colleges and universities have worked hard to make this a smooth process for older students. Many colleges have established special service offices that are staffed with trained professionals who understand the kinds of problems facing adults returning to college. If you think you might benefit from such assistance, be sure to find out whether these services are available at your college.

How to Apply for College Credit

STEP 1. Obtain the General Information Catalog and a copy of the CLEP policy from the colleges you are considering. If you have not yet applied for admission, ask for an admissions application form too.

Information about admissions and CLEP policies can be obtained by contacting college admissions offices or finding admissions information on the school websites. Tell the admissions officer that you are a prospective student and that you are interested in applying for admission and CLEP credit. Ask for a copy of the publication in which the college's complete CLEP policy is explained. Also get the name and the telephone number of the person to contact in case you have further questions about CLEP.

At this step, you may wish to obtain information from external degree colleges. Many adults find that such colleges suit their needs exceptionally well.

STEP 2. If you have not already been admitted to the college you are considering, look at its admission requirements for undergraduate students to see if you can qualify.

This is an important step because if you can't get into college, you can't get college credit for CLEP. Nearly all colleges require students to be admitted and to enroll in one or more courses before granting the students CLEP credit.

Virtually all public community colleges and a number of four-year state colleges have open admission policies for in-state students. This usually means that they admit anyone who has graduated from high school or has earned a high school equivalency diploma.

If you think you do not meet the admission requirements, contact the admissions office for an interview with a counselor. Colleges do sometimes make exceptions, particularly for adult applicants. State why you want the interview and ask what documents you should bring with you or send in advance. (These materials may include a high school transcript, transcript of previous college work, completed application for admission, etc.) Make an extra effort to have all the information requested in time for the interview.

During the interview, relax and be yourself. Be prepared to state honestly why you think you are ready and able to do college work. If you have already taken CLEP examinations and scored high enough to earn credit, you have shown that you are able to do college work. Mention this achievement to the admissions counselor because it may increase your chances of being accepted. If you have not taken a CLEP examination, you can still improve your chances of being accepted by describing how your job training or independent study has helped prepare you for college-level work. Tell the counselor what you have learned from your work and personal experiences.

STEP 3. Evaluate the college's CLEP policy.

Typically, a college lists all its academic policies, including CLEP policies, in its general catalog. You will probably find the CLEP policy statement under a heading such as Credit-by-Examination, Advanced Standing, Advanced Placement, or External Degree Program. These sections can usually be found in the front of the catalog.

Many colleges publish their credit-by-examination policies in a separate brochure, which is distributed through the campus testing office, counseling center, admissions office, or registrar's office. If you find a very general policy statement in the college catalog, seek clarification from one of these offices.

Review the material in the section of this guide entitled Questions to Ask About a College's CLEP Policy. Use these guidelines to evaluate the college's CLEP policy. If you have not yet taken a CLEP examination, this evaluation will help you decide which examinations to take and whether or not to take the free-response or essay portion. Because individual colleges have different CLEP policies, a review of several policies may help you decide which college to attend.

STEP 4. If you have not yet applied for admission, do so early.

Most colleges expect you to apply for admission several months before you enroll, and it is essential that you meet the published application deadlines. It takes time to process your application for admission; and if you have yet to take a CLEP examination, it will be some time before the college receives and reviews your score report. You will probably want to take some, if not all, of the CLEP examinations you are interested in before you enroll so you know which courses you need not register for. In fact, some colleges require that all CLEP scores be submitted before a student registers.

Complete all forms and include all documents requested with your application(s) for admission. Normally, an admissions decision cannot be reached until all documents have been submitted and evaluated. Unless told to do so, do not send your CLEP scores until you have been officially admitted.

STEP 5. Arrange to take CLEP examination(s) or to submit your CLEP score(s).

You may want to wait to take your CLEP examinations until you know definitely which college you will be attending. Then you can make sure you are taking tests your college will accept for credit. You will also be able to request that your scores be sent to the college, free of charge, when you take the tests.

If you have already taken CLEP examinations, but did not have a copy of your score report sent to your college, you may request the College Board to send an official transcript at any time for a small fee. Use the Transcript Request Form that was sent to you with your score report. If you do not have the form, you may find it online at www.collegeboard.com/clep.

Your CLEP scores will be evaluated, probably by someone in the admissions office, and sent to the registrar's office to be posted on your permanent record once you are enrolled. Procedures vary from college to college, but the process usually begins in the admissions office.

STEP 6. Ask to receive a written notice of the credit you receive for your CLEP score(s).

A written notice may save you problems later, when you submit your degree plan or file for graduation. In the event that there is a question about whether or not you earned CLEP credit, you will have an official record of what credit was awarded. You may also need this verification of course credit if you go for academic counseling before the credit is posted on your permanent record.

STEP 7. Before you register for courses, seek academic counseling.

A discussion with your academic advisor can prevent you from taking unnecessary courses and can tell you specifically what your CLEP credit will mean to you. This step may be accomplished at the time you enroll. Most colleges have orientation sessions for new students prior to each enrollment period. During orientation, students are usually assigned an academic advisor who then gives them individual help in developing long-range plans and a course schedule for the next semester. In conjunction with this counseling, you may be asked to take some additional tests so that you can be placed at the proper course level.

External Degree Programs

If you have acquired a considerable amount of college-level knowledge through job experience, reading, or noncredit courses, if you have accumulated college credits at a variety of colleges over a period of years, or if you prefer studying on your own rather than in a classroom setting, you may want to investigate the possibility of enrolling in an external degree program. Many colleges offer external degree programs that allow you to earn a degree by passing examinations (including CLEP), transferring credit from other colleges, and demonstrating in other ways that you have satisfied the educational requirements. No classroom attendance is required, and the programs are open to out-of-state candidates as well as residents. Thomas A. Edison State College in New Jersey and Charter Oaks College in Connecticut are fully accredited independent state colleges; the New York program is part of the state university system and is also fully accredited. If you are interested in exploring an external degree, you can write for more information to:

Charter Oak College
The Exchange, Suite 171
270 Farmington Avenue
Farmington, CT 06032-1909

Regents External Degree Program
Cultural Education Center
Empire State Plaza
Albany, New York 12230

Thomas A. Edison State College
101 West State Street
Trenton, New Jersey 08608

Many other colleges also have external degree or weekend programs. While they often require that a number of courses be taken on campus, the external degree programs tend to be more flexible in transferring credit, granting credit-by-examination, and allowing independent study than other traditional programs. When applying to a college, you may wish to ask whether it has an external degree or weekend program.

Questions to Ask About a College's CLEP Policy

Before taking CLEP examinations for the purpose of earning college credit, try to find the answers to these questions:

1. Which CLEP examinations are accepted by this college?

A college may accept some CLEP examinations for credit and not others - possibly not the one you are considering. The English faculty may decide to grant college English credit based on the CLEP English Composition examination, but not on the Freshman College Composition examination. Or, the mathematics faculty may decide to grant credit based on the College Mathematics to non-mathematics majors only, requiring majors to take an examination in algebra, trigonometry, or calculus to earn credit. For these reasons, it is important that you know the specific CLEP tests for which you can receive credit.

2. Does the college require the optional free-response (essay) section as well as the objective portion of the CLEP examination you are considering?

Knowing the answer to this question ahead of time will permit you to schedule the optional essay examination when you register to take your CLEP examination.

3. Is credit granted for specific courses? If so, which ones?

You are likely to find that credit will be granted for specific courses and the course titles will be designated in the college's CLEP policy. It is not necessary, however, that credit be granted for a specific course in order for you to benefit from your CLEP credit. For instance, at many liberal arts colleges, all students must take certain types of courses; these courses may be labeled the core curriculum, general education requirements, distribution requirements, or liberal arts requirements. The requirements are often expressed in terms of credit hours. For example, all students may be required to take at least six hours of humanities, six hours of English, three hours of mathematics, six hours of natural science, and six hours of social science, with no particular courses in these disciplines specified. In these instances, CLEP credit may be given as 6 hrs. English credit or 3 hrs. Math credit without specifying for which English or mathematics courses credit has been awarded. In order to avoid possible disappointment, you should know before taking a CLEP examination what type of credit you can receive and whether you will only be exempted from a required course but receive no credit.

4. How much credit is granted for each examination you are considering, and does the college place a limit on the total amount of CLEP credit you can earn toward your degree?

Not all colleges that grant CLEP credit award the same amount for individual tests. Furthermore, some colleges place a limit on the total amount of credit you can earn through CLEP or other examinations. Other colleges may grant you exemption but no credit toward your degree. Knowing several colleges' policies concerning these issues may help you decide which college you will attend. If you think you are capable of passing a number of CLEP examinations, you may want to attend a college that will allow you to earn credit for all or most of them. For example, the state external degree programs grant credit for most CLEP examinations (and other tests as well).

5. What is the required score for earning CLEP credit for each test you are considering?

Most colleges publish the required scores or percentile ranks for earning CLEP credit in their general catalog or in a brochure. The required score may vary from test to test, so find out the required score for each test you are considering.

6. What is the college's policy regarding prior course work in the subject in which you are considering taking a CLEP test?

Some colleges will not grant credit for a CLEP test if the student has already attempted a college-level course closely aligned with that test. For example, if you successfully completed English 101 or a comparable course on another campus, you will probably not be permitted to receive CLEP credit in that subject, too. Some colleges will not permit you to earn CLEP credit for a course that you failed.

7. Does the college make additional stipulations before credit will be granted?

It is common practice for colleges to award CLEP credit only to their enrolled students. There are other stipulations, however, that vary from college to college. For example, does the college require you to formally apply for or accept CLEP credit by completing and signing a form? Or does the college require you to validate your CLEP score by successfully completing a more advanced course in the subject? Answers to these and other questions will help to smooth the process of earning college credit through CLEP.

The above questions and the discussions that follow them indicate some of the ways in which colleges' CLEP policies can vary. Find out as much as possible about the CLEP policies at the colleges you are interested in so you can choose a college with a policy that is compatible with your educational goals. Once you have selected the college you will attend, you can find out which CLEP examinations your college recognizes and the requirements for earning CLEP credit.

DECIDING WHICH EXAMINATIONS TO TAKE

If You're Taking the Examinations for College Credit or Career Advancement:

Most people who take CLEP examinations do so in order to earn credit for college courses. Others take the examinations in order to qualify for job promotions or for professional certification or licensing. It is vital to most candidates who are taking the tests for any of these reasons that they be well prepared for the tests they are taking so that they can advance as rapidly as possible toward their educational or career goals.

It is usually advisable that those who have limited knowledge in the subjects covered by the tests they are considering enroll in the college courses in which that material is taught. Those who are uncertain about whether or not they know enough about a subject to do well on a particular CLEP test will find the following guidelines helpful.

There is no way to predict if you will pass a particular CLEP examination, but answers to the questions under the seven headings below should give you an indication of whether or not you are likely to succeed.

1. Test Descriptions

Read the description of the test provided. Are you familiar with most of the topics and terminology in the outline?

2. Textbooks

Examine the suggested textbooks and other resource materials following the test descriptions in this guide. Have you recently read one or more of these books, or have you read similar college-level books on this subject? If you have not, read through one or more of the textbooks listed, or through the textbook used for this course at your college. Are you familiar with most of the topics and terminology in the book?

3. Sample Questions

The sample questions provided are intended to be typical of the content and difficulty of the questions on the test. Although they are not an exact miniature of the test, the proportion of the sample questions you can answer correctly should be a rough estimate of the proportion of questions you will be able to answer correctly on the test.

Answer as many of the sample questions for this test as you can. Check your answers against the correct answers. Did you answer more than half the questions correctly?

Because of variations in course content at different institutions, and because questions on CLEP tests vary from easy to difficult - with most being of moderate difficulty - the average student who passes a course in a subject can usually answer correctly about half the questions on the corresponding CLEP examination. Most colleges set their passing scores near this level, but some set them higher. If your college has set its required score above the level required by most colleges, you may need to answer a larger proportion of questions on the test correctly.

4. Previous Study

Have you taken noncredit courses in this subject offered by an adult school or a private school, through correspondence, or in connection with your job? Did you do exceptionally well in this subject in high school, or did you take an honors course in this subject?

5. Experience

Have you learned or used the knowledge or skills included in this test in your job or life experience? For example, if you lived in a Spanish-speaking country and spoke the language for a year or more, you might consider taking the Spanish examination. Or, if you have worked at a job in which you used accounting and finance skills, Principles of Accounting would be a likely test for you to take. Or, if you have read a considerable amount of literature and attended many art exhibits, concerts, and plays, you might expect to do well on the Humanities exam.

6. Other Examinations

Have you done well on other standardized tests in subjects related to the one you want to take? For example, did you score well above average on a portion of a college entrance examination covering similar skills, or did you obtain an exceptionally high score on a high school equivalency test or a licensing examination in this subject? Although such tests do not cover exactly the same material as the CLEP examinations and may be easier, persons who do well on these tests often do well on CLEP examinations, too.

7. Advice

Has a college counselor, professor, or some other professional person familiar with your ability advised you to take a CLEP examination?

If your answer was yes to questions under several of the above headings, you probably have a good chance of passing the CLEP examination you are considering. It is unlikely that you would have acquired sufficient background from experience alone. Learning gained through reading and study is essential, and you will probably find some additional study helpful before taking a CLEP examination.

If You're Taking the Examinations to Prepare for College

Many people entering college, particularly adults returning to college after several years away from formal education, are uncertain about their ability to compete with other college students. They wonder whether they have sufficient background for college study, and those who have been away from formal study for some time wonder whether they have forgotten how to study, how to take tests, and how to write papers. Such people may wish to improve their test-taking and study skills prior to enrolling in courses.

One way to assess your ability to perform at the college level and to improve your test-taking and study skills at the same time is to prepare for and take one or more CLEP examinations. You need not be enrolled in a college to take a CLEP examination, and you may have your scores sent only to yourself and later request that a transcript be sent to a college if you then decide to apply for credit. By reviewing the test descriptions and sample questions, you may find one or several subject areas in which you think you have substantial knowledge. Select one examination, or more if you like, and carefully read at least one of the textbooks listed in the bibliography for the test. By doing this, you will get a better idea of how much you know of what is usually taught in a college-level course in that subject. Study as much material as you can, until you think you have a good grasp of the subject matter. Then take the test at a college in your area. It will be several weeks before you receive your results, and you may wish to begin reviewing for another test in the meantime.

To find out if you are eligible for credit for your CLEP score, you must compare your score with the score required by the college you plan to attend. If you are not yet sure which college you will attend, or whether you will enroll in college at all, you should begin to follow the steps outlined. It is best that you do this before taking a CLEP test, but if you are taking the test only for the experience and to familiarize yourself with college-level material and requirements, you might take the test before you approach a college. Even if the college you decide to attend does not accept the test you took, the experience of taking such a test will enable you to meet with greater confidence the requirements of courses you will take.

You will find information about how to interpret your scores in WHAT YOUR SCORES MEAN, which you will receive with your score report, and which can also be found online at the CLEP website. Many colleges follow the recommendations of the American Council on Education (ACE) for setting their required scores, so you can use this information as a guide in determining how well you did. The ACE recommendations are included in the booklet.

If you do not do well enough on the test to earn college credit, don't be discouraged. Usually, it is the best college students who are exempted from courses or receive credit-by-examination. The fact that you cannot get credit for your score means that you should probably enroll in a college course to learn the material. However, if your score was close to the required score, or if you feel you could do better on a second try or after some additional study, you may retake the test after six months. Do not take it sooner or your score will not be reported and your fee will be forfeited.

If you do earn the score required to earn credit, you will have demonstrated that you already have some college-level knowledge. You will also have a better idea whether you should take additional CLEP examinations. And, what is most important, you can enroll in college with confidence, knowing that you do have the ability to succeed.

PREPARING TO TAKE CLEP EXAMINATIONS

Having made the decision to take one or more CLEP examinations, most people then want to know if it is worthwhile to prepare for them - how much, how long, when, and how should they go about it? The precise answers to these questions vary greatly from individual to individual. However, most candidates find that some type of test preparation is helpful.

Most people who take CLEP examinations do so to show that they have already learned the important material that is taught in a college course. Many of them need only a quick review to assure themselves that they have not forgotten some of what they once studied, and to fill in some of the gaps in their knowledge of the subject. Others feel that they need a thorough review and spend several weeks studying for a test. A few wish to take a CLEP examination as a kind of final examination for independent study of a subject instead of the college course. This last group requires significantly more study than those who only need to review, and they may need some guidance from professors of the subjects they are studying.

The key to how you prepare for CLEP examinations often lies in locating those skills and areas of prior learning in which you are strong and deciding where to focus your energies. Some people may know a great deal about a certain subject area, but may not test well. These individuals would probably be just as concerned about strengthening their test-taking skills as they are about studying for a specific test. Many mental and physical skills are used in preparing for a test. It is important not only to review or study for the examinations, but to make certain that you are alert, relatively free of anxiety, and aware of how to approach standardized tests. Suggestions on developing test-taking skills and preparing psychologically and physically for a test are given. The following section suggests ways of assessing your knowledge of the content of a test and then reviewing and studying the material.

Using This Study Guide

Begin by carefully reading the test description and outline of knowledge and skills required for the examination, if given. As you read through the topics listed there, ask yourself how much you know about each one. Also note the terms, names, and symbols that are mentioned, and ask yourself whether you are familiar with them. This will give you a quick overview of how much you know about the subject. If you are familiar with nearly all the material, you will probably need a minimum of review; however, if less than half of it is familiar, you will probably require substantial study to do well on the test.

If, after reviewing the test description, you find that you need extensive review, delay answering the sample question until you have done some reading in the subject. If you complete them before reviewing the material, you will probably look for the answers as you study, and then they will not be a good assessment of your ability at a later date.

If you think you are familiar with most of the test material, try to answer the sample questions.

Apply the test-taking strategies given. Keeping within the time limit suggested will give you a rough idea of how quickly you should work in order to complete the actual test.

Check your answers against the answer key. If you answered nearly all the questions correctly, you probably do not need to study the subject extensively. If you got about half the questions correct, you ought o review at least one textbook or other suggested materials on the subject. If you answered less than half the questions correctly, you will probably benefit from more extensive reading in the subject and thorough study of one or more textbooks. The textbooks listed are used at many colleges but they are not the only good texts. You will find helpful almost any standard text available to you., such as the textbook used at your college, or earlier editions of texts listed. For some examinations, topic outlines and textbooks may not be available. Take the sample tests in this book and check your answers at the end of each test. Check wrong answers.

Suggestions for Studying

The following suggestions have been gathered from people who have prepared for CLEP examinations or other college-level tests.

1. Define your goals and locate study materials

First, determine your study goals. Set aside a block of time to review the material provided in this book, and then decide which test(s) you will take. Using the suggestions, locate suitable resource materials. If a preparation course is offered by an adult school or college in your area, you might find it helpful to enroll.

2. Find a good place to study

To determine what kind of place you need for studying, ask yourself questions such as: Do I need a quiet place? Does the telephone distract me? Do objects I see in this place remind me of things I should do? Is it too warm? Is it well lit? Am I too comfortable here? Do I have space to spread out my materials? You may find the library more conducive to studying than your home. If you decide to study at home, you might prevent interruptions by other household members by putting a sign on the door of your study room to indicate when you will be available.

3. Schedule time to study

To help you determine where studying best fits into your schedule, try this exercise: Make a list of your daily activities (for example, sleeping, working, and eating) and estimate how many hours per day you spend on each activity. Now, rate all the activities on your list in order of their importance and evaluate your use of time. Often people are astonished at how an average day appears from this perspective. They may discover that they were unaware how large portions of time are spent, or they learn their time can be scheduled in alternative ways. For example, they can remove the least important activities from their day and devote that time to studying or another important activity.

4. Establish a study routine and a set of goals

In order to study effectively, you should establish specific goals and a schedule for accomplishing them. Some people find it helpful to write out a weekly schedule and cross out each study period when it is completed. Others maintain their concentration better by writing down the time when they expect to complete a study task. Most people find short periods of intense study more productive than long stretches of time. For example, they may follow a regular schedule of several 20- or 30-minute study periods with short breaks between them. Some people like to allow themselves rewards as they complete each study goal. It is not essential that you accomplish every goal exactly within your schedule; the point is to be committed to your task.

5. Learn how to take an active role in studying.

If you have not done much studying for some time, you may find it difficult to concentrate at first. Try a method of studying, such as the one outlined below, that will help you concentrate on and remember what you read.

    a. First, read the chapter summary and the introduction. Then you will know what to look for in your reading.

    b. Next, convert the section or paragraph headlines into questions. For example, if you are reading a section entitled, The Causes of the American Revolution, ask yourself: *What were the causes of the American Revolution?* Compose the answer as you read the paragraph. Reading and answering questions aloud will help you understand and remember the material.

c. Take notes on key ideas or concepts as you read. Writing will also help you fix concepts more firmly in your mind. Underlining key ideas or writing notes in your book can be helpful and will be useful for review. Underline only important points. If you underline more than a third of each paragraph, you are probably underlining too much.

d. If there are questions or problems at the end of a chapter, answer or solve them on paper as if you were asked to do them for homework. Mathematics textbooks (and some other books) sometimes include answers to some or all of the exercises. If you have such a book, write your answers before looking at the ones given. When problem-solving is involved, work enough problems to master the required methods and concepts. If you have difficulty with problems, review any sample problems or explanations in the chapter.

e. To retain knowledge, most people have to review the material periodically. If you are preparing for a test over an extended period of time, review key concepts and notes each week or so. Do not wait for weeks to review the material or you will need to relearn much of it.

Psychological and Physical Preparation

Most people feel at least some nervousness before taking a test. Adults who are returning to college may not have taken a test in many years or they may have had little experience with standardized tests. Some younger students, as well, are uncomfortable with testing situations. People who received their education in countries outside the United States may find that many tests given in this country are quite different from the ones they are accustomed to taking.

Not only might candidates find the types of tests and the kinds of questions on them unfamiliar, but other aspects of the testing environment may be strange as well. The physical and mental stress that results from meeting this new experience can hinder a candidate's ability to demonstrate his or her true degree of knowledge in the subject area being tested. For this reason, it is important to go to the test center well prepared, both mentally and physically, for taking the test. You may find the following suggestions helpful.

1. Familiarize yourself, as much as possible, with the test and the test situation before the day of the examination. It will be helpful for you to know ahead of time:

a. How much time will be allowed for the test and whether there are timed subsections.

b. What types of questions and directions appear on the examination.

c. How your test score will be computed.

d. How to properly answer the questions on the computer (See the CLEP Sample on the CLEP website)

e. In which building and room the examination will be administered. If you don't know where the building is, locate it or get directions ahead of time.

f. The time of the test administration. You might wish to confirm this information a day or two before the examination and find out what time the building and room will be open so that you can plan to arrive early.

g. Where to park your car or, if you wish to take public transportation, which bus or train to take and the location of the nearest stop.

h. Whether smoking will be permitted during the test.

i. Whether there will be a break between examinations (if you will be taking more than one on the same day), and whether there is a place nearby where you can get something to eat or drink.

2. Go to the test situation relaxed and alert. In order to prepare for the test:

a. Get a good night's sleep. Last minute cramming, particularly late the night before, is usually counterproductive.

b. Eat normally. It is usually not wise to skip breakfast or lunch on the day of the test or to eat a big meal just before the test.

c. Avoid tranquilizers and stimulants. If you follow the other directions in this book, you won't need artificial aids. It's better to be a little tense than to be drowsy, but stimulants such as coffee and cola can make you nervous and interfere with your concentration.

d. Don't drink a lot of liquids before the test. Having to leave the room during the test will disturb your concentration and take valuable time away from the test.

e. If you are inclined to be nervous or tense, learn some relaxation exercises and use them before and perhaps during the test.

3. Arrive for the test early and prepared. Be sure to:

a. Arrive early enough so that you can find a parking place, locate the test center, and get settled comfortably before testing begins. Allow some extra time in case you are delayed unexpectedly.

b. Take the following with you:

- Your completed Registration/Admission Form
- Two forms of identification – one being a government-issued photo ID with signature, such as a driver's license or passport
- Non-mechanical pencil
- A watch so that you can time your progress (digital watches are prohibited)
- Your glasses if you need them for reading or seeing the chalkboard or wall clock

  c. Leave all books, papers, and notes outside the test center. You will not be permitted to use your own scratch paper; it will be provided. Also prohibited are calculators, cell phones, beepers, pagers, photo/copy devices, radios, headphones, food, beverages, and several other items.

  d. Be prepared for any temperature in the testing room. Wear layers of clothing that can be removed if the room is too hot but will keep you warm if it is too cold.

4. When you enter the test room:

  a. Sit in a seat that provides a maximum of comfort and freedom from distraction.

  b. Read directions carefully, and listen to all instructions given by the test administrator. If you don't understand the directions, ask for help before test timing begins. If you must ask a question after the test has begun, raise your hand and a proctor will assist you. The proctor can answer certain kinds of questions but cannot help you with the test.

  c. Know your rights as a test taker. You can expect to be given the full working time allowed for the test(s) and a reasonably quiet and comfortable place in which to work. If a poor test situation is preventing you from doing your best, ask if the situation can be remedied. If bad test conditions cannot be remedied, ask the person in charge to report the problem in the Irregularity Report that will be sent to ETS with the answer sheets. You may also wish to contact CLEP. Describe the exact circumstances as completely as you can. Be sure to include the test date and name(s) of the test(s) you took. ETS will investigate the problem to make sure it does not happen again, and, if the problem is serious enough, may arrange for you to retake the test without charge.

TAKING THE EXAMINATIONS

A person may know a great deal about the subject being tested, but not do as well as he or she is capable of on the test. Knowing how to approach a test is an important part of the testing process. While a command of test-taking skills cannot substitute for knowledge of the subject matter, it can be a significant factor in successful testing.

Test-taking skills enable a person to use all available information to earn a score that truly reflects his or her ability. There are different strategies for approaching different kinds of test questions. For example, free-response questions require a very different tack than do multiple-choice questions. Other factors, such as how the test will be graded, may also influence your approach to the test and your use of test time. Thus, your preparation for a test should include finding out all you can about the test so that you can use the most effective test-taking strategies.

Before taking a test, you should know approximately how many questions are on the test, how much time you will be allowed, how the test will be scored or graded, what types of questions and directions are on the test, and how you will be required to record your answers.

Taking Multiple-Choice Tests

1. Listen carefully to the instructions given by the test administrator and read carefully all directions before you begin to answer the questions.

2. Note the time that the test administrator starts timing the test. As you proceed, make sure that you are not working too slowly. You should have answered at least half the questions in a section when half the time for that section has passed. If you have not reached that point in the section, speed up your pace on the remaining questions.

3. Before answering a question, read the entire question, including all the answer choices. Don't think that because the first or second answer choice looks good to you, it isn't necessary to read the remaining options. Instructions usually tell you to select the best answer. Sometimes one answer choice is partially correct, but another option is better; therefore, it is usually a good idea to read all the answers before you choose one.

4. Read and consider every question. Questions that look complicated at first glance may not actually be so difficult once you have read them carefully.

5. Do not puzzle too long over any one question. If you don't know the answer after you've considered it briefly, go on to the next question. Make sure you return to the question later.

6. Make sure you record your response properly.

7. In trying to determine the correct answer, you may find it helpful to cross out those options that you know are incorrect, and to make marks next to those you think might be correct. If you decide to skip the question and come back to it later, you will save yourself the time of reconsidering all the options.

8. Watch for the following key words in test questions:

all	generally	never	perhaps
always	however	none	rarely
but	may	not	seldom
except	must	often	sometimes
every	necessary	only	usually

When a question or answer option contains words such as always, every, only, never, and none, there can be no exceptions to the answer you choose. Use of words such as often, rarely, sometimes, and generally indicates that there may be some exceptions to the answer.

9. Do not waste your time looking for clues to right answers based on flaws in question wording or patterns in correct answers. Professionals at the College Board and ETS put

a great deal of effort into developing valid, reliable, fair tests. CLEP test development committees are composed of college faculty who are experts in the subject covered by the test and are appointed by the College Board to write test questions and to scrutinize each question that is included on a CLEP test. Committee members make every effort to ensure that the questions are not ambiguous, that they have only one correct answer, and that they cover college-level topics. These committees do not intentionally include trick questions. If you think a question is flawed, ask the test administrator to report it, or contact CLEP immediately.

Taking Free-Response or Essay Tests

If your college requires the optional free-response or essay portion of a CLEP Composition and Literature exams, you should do some additional preparation for your CLEP test. Taking an essay test is very different from taking a multiple-choice test, so you will need to use some other strategies.

The essay written as part of the English Composition and Essay exam is graded by English professors from a variety of colleges and universities. A process called holistic scoring is used to rate your writing ability.

The optional free-response essays, on the other hand, are graded by the faculty of the college you designate as a score recipient. Guidelines and criteria for grading essays are not specified by the College Board or ETS. You may find it helpful, therefore, to talk with someone at your college to find out what criteria will be used to determine whether you will get credit. If the test requires essay responses, ask how much emphasis will be placed on your writing ability and your ability to organize your thoughts as opposed to your knowledge of subject matter. Find out how much weight will be given to your multiple-choice test score in comparison with your free-response grade in determining whether you will get credit. This will give you an idea where you should expend the greatest effort in preparing for and taking the test.

Here are some strategies you will find useful in taking any essay test:

1. Before you begin to write, read all questions carefully and take a few minutes to jot down some ideas you might include in each answer.

2. If you are given a choice of questions to answer, choose the questions you think you can answer most clearly and knowledgeably.

3. Determine in what order you will answer the questions. Answer those you find the easiest first so that any extra time can be spent on the more difficult questions.

4. When you know which questions you will answer and in what order, determine how much testing time remains and estimate how many minutes you will devote to each question. Unless suggested times are given for the questions or one question appears to require more or less time than the others, allot an equal amount of time to each question.

5. Before answering each question, indicate the number of the question as it is given in the test book. You need not copy the entire question from the question sheet, but it will be helpful to you and to the person grading your test if you indicate briefly the topic you are addressing – particularly if you are not answering the questions in the order in which they appear on the test.

6. Before answering each question, read it again carefully to make sure you are interpreting it correctly. Underline key words, such as those listed below, that often appear in free-response questions. Be sure you know the exact meaning of these words before taking the test.

analyze	demonstrate	enumerate	list
apply	derive	explain	outline
assess	describe	generalize	prove
compare	determine	illustrate	rank
contrast	discuss	interpret	show
define	distinguish	justify	summarize

If a question asks you to outline, define, or summarize, do not write a detailed explanation; if a question asks you to analyze, explain, illustrate, interpret, or show, you must do more than briefly describe the topic.

For a current listing of CLEP Colleges

where you can get credit and be tested, write:

CLEP, P.O. Box 6600, Princeton, NJ 08541-6600

Or e-mail: clep@ets.org, or call: (609) 771-7865

Analysis and Interpretation of Literature

Description of the Examination
The Analyzing and Interpreting Literature examination covers material usually taught in a general two-semester undergraduate course in literature. Although the examination does not require familiarity with specific works, it does assume that candidates have read widely and perceptively in poetry, drama, fiction, and nonfiction. The questions are based on passages supplied in the test. These passages have been selected so that no previous experience with them is required to answer the questions. The passages are taken primarily from American and British literature.

The examination contains approximately 80 multiple choice questions to be answered in 90 minutes. Some of these are pretest questions that will not be scored. Any time candidates spend taking tutorials and providing personal information is additional to actual testing time.

Because writing about literary texts is central to the study of literature, some colleges may require candidates to take an optional essay section in addition to the multiple-choice section. The essay section is 90 minutes long and is made up of two 45-minute questions. One question asks candidates to analyze a short poem, the other asks them to apply a given generalization about literature (such as the function of a theme or a technique) to a novel, short story, or play that they have read. The essay section is still administered in a paper-and-pencil format; the essay responses are graded by the institution, not by the College Board.

Knowledge and Skills Required
Questions on the Analyzing and Interpreting Literature examination require candidates to demonstrate the following abilities.

- Ability to read prose, poetry, and drama with understanding
- Ability to analyze the elements of a literary passage and to respond to nuances of meaning, tone, imagery, and style Ability to interpret metaphors, to recognize rhetorical and stylistic devices, to perceive relationships between parts and wholes, and to grasp a speaker's or author's attitudes
- Knowledge of the means by which literary effects are achieved
- Familiarity with the basic terminology used to discuss literary texts

The examination emphasizes comprehension, interpretation, and analysis of literary works. A specific knowledge of historical context (authors and movements) is not required, but a broad knowledge of literature gained through reading widely and a familiarity with basic literary terminology is assumed. The following outline indicates the relative emphasis given to the various types of literature and the periods from which the passages are taken. The approximate percentage of exam questions per classification is noted within each main category.

From the official announcement for educational purposes

Genre
35-45% Poetry
35-45% Prose (fiction and nonfiction)
15-30% Drama

National Tradition
50-65% British Literature
30-45% American Literature
5-15% Works in translation

Period
3-7% Classical and pre-Renaissance
20-30% Renaissance and 17th Century
35-45% 18th and 19th Centuries
25-35% 20th and 21st Centuries

HOW TO TAKE A TEST

You have studied long, hard and conscientiously.

With your official admission card in hand, and your heart pounding, you have been admitted to the examination room.

You note that there are several hundred other applicants in the examination room waiting to take the same test.

They all appear to be equally well prepared.

You know that nothing but your best effort will suffice. The "moment of truth" is at hand: you now have to demonstrate objectively, in writing, your knowledge of content and your understanding of subject matter.

You are fighting the most important battle of your life—to pass and/or score high on an examination which will determine your career and provide the economic basis for your livelihood.

What extra, special things should you know and should you do in taking the examination?

I. YOU MUST PASS AN EXAMINATION

A. WHAT EVERY CANDIDATE SHOULD KNOW

Examination applicants often ask us for help in preparing for the written test. What can I study in advance? What kinds of questions will be asked? How will the test be given? How will the papers be graded?

B. HOW ARE EXAMS DEVELOPED?

Examinations are carefully written by trained technicians who are specialists in the field known as "psychological measurement," in consultation with recognized authorities in the field of work that the test will cover. These experts recommend the subject matter areas or skills to be tested; only those knowledges or skills important to your success on the job are included. The most reliable books and source materials available are used as references. Together, the experts and technicians judge the difficulty level of the questions.

Test technicians know how to phrase questions so that the problem is clearly stated. Their ethics do not permit "trick" or "catch" questions. Questions may have been tried out on sample groups, or subjected to statistical analysis, to determine their usefulness.

Written tests are often used in combination with performance tests, ratings of training and experience, and oral interviews. All of these measures combine to form the best-known means of finding the right person for the right job.

II. HOW TO PASS THE WRITTEN TEST

A. BASIC STEPS

1) Study the announcement

How, then, can you know what subjects to study? Our best answer is: "Learn as much as possible about the class of positions for which you've applied." The exam will test the knowledge, skills and abilities needed to do the work.

Your most valuable source of information about the position you want is the official exam announcement. This announcement lists the training and experience qualifications. Check these standards and apply only if you come reasonably close to meeting them. Many jurisdictions preview the written test in the exam announcement by including a section called "Knowledge and Abilities Required," "Scope of the Examination," or some similar heading. Here you will find out specifically what fields will be tested.

2) Choose appropriate study materials

If the position for which you are applying is technical or advanced, you will read more advanced, specialized material. If you are already familiar with the basic principles of your field, elementary textbooks would waste your time. Concentrate on advanced textbooks and technical periodicals. Think through the concepts and review difficult problems in your field.

These are all general sources. You can get more ideas on your own initiative, following these leads. For example, training manuals and publications of the government agency which employs workers in your field can be useful, particularly for technical and professional positions. A letter or visit to the government department involved may result in more specific study suggestions, and certainly will provide you with a more definite idea of the exact nature of the position you are seeking.

3) Study this book!

III. KINDS OF TESTS

Tests are used for purposes other than measuring knowledge and ability to perform specified duties. For some positions, it is equally important to test ability to make adjustments to new situations or to profit from training. In others, basic mental abilities not dependent on information are essential. Questions which test these things may not appear as pertinent to the duties of the position as those which test for knowledge and information. Yet they are often highly important parts of a fair examination. For very general questions, it is almost impossible to help you direct your study efforts. What we can do is to point out some of the more common of these general abilities needed in public service positions and describe some typical questions.

1) General information

Broad, general information has been found useful for predicting job success in some kinds of work. This is tested in a variety of ways, from vocabulary lists to questions about current events. Basic background in some field of work, such as sociology or economics, may be sampled in a group of questions. Often these are principles which have become familiar to most persons through exposure rather than through formal training. It is difficult to advise you how to study for these questions; being alert to the world around you is our best suggestion.

2) Verbal ability

An example of an ability needed in many positions is verbal or language ability. Verbal ability is, in brief, the ability to use and understand words. Vocabulary and grammar tests are typical measures of this ability. Reading comprehension or paragraph interpretation questions are common in many kinds of civil service tests. You are given a paragraph of written material and asked to find its central meaning.

IV. KINDS OF QUESTIONS

1. Multiple-choice Questions

Most popular of the short-answer questions is the "multiple choice" or "best answer" question. It can be used, for example, to test for factual knowledge, ability to solve problems or judgment in meeting situations found at work.

A multiple-choice question is normally one of three types:
- It can begin with an incomplete statement followed by several possible endings. You are to find the one ending which *best* completes the statement, although some of the others may not be entirely wrong.
- It can also be a complete statement in the form of a question which is answered by choosing one of the statements listed.
- It can be in the form of a problem – again you select the best answer.

Here is an example of a multiple-choice question with a discussion which should give you some clues as to the method for choosing the right answer:

When an employee has a complaint about his assignment, the action which will *best* help him overcome his difficulty is to
    A. discuss his difficulty with his coworkers
    B. take the problem to the head of the organization
    C. take the problem to the person who gave him the assignment
    D. say nothing to anyone about his complaint

In answering this question, you should study each of the choices to find which is best. Consider choice "A" – Certainly an employee may discuss his complaint with fellow employees, but no change or improvement can result, and the complaint remains unresolved. Choice "B" is a poor choice since the head of the organization probably does not know what assignment you have been given, and taking your problem to him is known as "going over the head" of the supervisor. The supervisor, or person who made the assignment, is the person who can clarify it or correct any injustice. Choice "C" is, therefore, correct. To say nothing, as in choice "D," is unwise. Supervisors have and interest in knowing the problems employees are facing, and the employee is seeking a solution to his problem.

2. True/False

3. Matching Questions
Matching an answer from a column of choices within another column.

V. RECORDING YOUR ANSWERS

Computer terminals are used more and more today for many different kinds of exams.

For an examination with very few applicants, you may be told to record your answers in the test booklet itself. Separate answer sheets are much more common. If this separate answer sheet is to be scored by machine – and this is often the case – it is highly important that you mark your answers correctly in order to get credit.

VI. BEFORE THE TEST

YOUR PHYSICAL CONDITION IS IMPORTANT
If you are not well, you can't do your best work on tests. If you are half asleep, you can't do your best either. Here are some tips:

1) Get about the same amount of sleep you usually get. Don't stay up all night before the test, either partying or worrying—DON'T DO IT!
2) If you wear glasses, be sure to wear them when you go to take the test. This goes for hearing aids, too.
3) If you have any physical problems that may keep you from doing your best, be sure to tell the person giving the test. If you are sick or in poor health, you relay cannot do your best on any test. You can always come back and take the test some other time.

Common sense will help you find procedures to follow to get ready for an examination. Too many of us, however, overlook these sensible measures. Indeed, nervousness and fatigue have been found to be the most serious reasons why applicants fail to do their best on civil service tests. Here is a list of reminders:

- Begin your preparation early – Don't wait until the last minute to go scurrying around for books and materials or to find out what the position is all about.
- Prepare continuously – An hour a night for a week is better than an all-night cram session. This has been definitely established. What is more, a night a week for a month will return better dividends than crowding your study into a shorter period of time.
- Locate the place of the exam – You have been sent a notice telling you when and where to report for the examination. If the location is in a different town or otherwise unfamiliar to you, it would be well to inquire the best route and learn something about the building.
- Relax the night before the test – Allow your mind to rest. Do not study at all that night. Plan some mild recreation or diversion; then go to bed early and get a good night's sleep.
- Get up early enough to make a leisurely trip to the place for the test – This way unforeseen events, traffic snarls, unfamiliar buildings, etc. will not upset you.

- Dress comfortably – A written test is not a fashion show. You will be known by number and not by name, so wear something comfortable.
- Leave excess paraphernalia at home – Shopping bags and odd bundles will get in your way. You need bring only the items mentioned in the official notice you received; usually everything you need is provided. Do not bring reference books to the exam. They will only confuse those last minutes and be taken away from you when in the test room.
- Arrive somewhat ahead of time – If because of transportation schedules you must get there very early, bring a newspaper or magazine to take your mind off yourself while waiting.
- Locate the examination room – When you have found the proper room, you will be directed to the seat or part of the room where you will sit. Sometimes you are given a sheet of instructions to read while you are waiting. Do not fill out any forms until you are told to do so; just read them and be prepared.
- Relax and prepare to listen to the instructions
- If you have any physical problem that may keep you from doing your best, be sure to tell the test administrator. If you are sick or in poor health, you really cannot do your best on the exam. You can come back and take the test some other time.

VII. AT THE TEST

The day of the test is here and you have the test booklet in your hand. The temptation to get going is very strong. Caution! There is more to success than knowing the right answers. You must know how to identify your papers and understand variations in the type of short-answer question used in this particular examination. Follow these suggestions for maximum results from your efforts:

1) Cooperate with the monitor

The test administrator has a duty to create a situation in which you can be as much at ease as possible. He will give instructions, tell you when to begin, check to see that you are marking your answer sheet correctly, and so on. He is not there to guard you, although he will see that your competitors do not take unfair advantage. He wants to help you do your best.

2) Listen to all instructions

Don't jump the gun! Wait until you understand all directions. In most civil service tests you get more time than you need to answer the questions. So don't be in a hurry. Read each word of instructions until you clearly understand the meaning. Study the examples, listen to all announcements and follow directions. Ask questions if you do not understand what to do.

3) Identify your papers

Civil service exams are usually identified by number only. You will be assigned a number; you must not put your name on your test papers. Be sure to copy your number correctly. Since more than one exam may be given, copy your exact examination title.

4) Plan your time

Unless you are told that a test is a "speed" or "rate of work" test, speed itself is usually not important. Time enough to answer all the questions will be provided, but this does not mean that you have all day. An overall time limit has been set. Divide the total time (in minutes) by the number of questions to determine the approximate time you have for each question.

5) Do not linger over difficult questions

If you come across a difficult question, mark it with a paper clip (useful to have along) and come back to it when you have been through the booklet. One caution if you do this – be sure to skip a number on your answer sheet as well. Check often to be sure that you have not lost your place and that you are marking in the row numbered the same as the question you are answering.

6) Read the questions

Be sure you know what the question asks! Many capable people are unsuccessful because they failed to *read* the questions correctly.

7) Answer all questions

Unless you have been instructed that a penalty will be deducted for incorrect answers, it is better to guess than to omit a question.

8) Speed tests

It is often better NOT to guess on speed tests. It has been found that on timed tests people are tempted to spend the last few seconds before time is called in marking answers at random – without even reading them – in the hope of picking up a few extra points. To discourage this practice, the instructions may warn you that your score will be "corrected" for guessing. That is, a penalty will be applied. The incorrect answers will be deducted from the correct ones, or some other penalty formula will be used.

9) Review your answers

If you finish before time is called, go back to the questions you guessed or omitted to give them further thought. Review other answers if you have time.

10) Return your test materials

If you are ready to leave before others have finished or time is called, take ALL your materials to the monitor and leave quietly. Never take any test material with you. The monitor can discover whose papers are not complete, and taking a test booklet may be grounds for disqualification.

VIII. EXAMINATION TECHNIQUES

1) Read the general instructions carefully. These are usually printed on the first page of the exam booklet. As a rule, these instructions refer to the timing of the examination; the fact that you should not start work until the signal and must stop work at a signal, etc. If there are any *special* instructions, such as a choice of questions to be answered, make sure that you note this instruction carefully.

2) When you are ready to start work on the examination, that is as soon as the signal has been given, read the instructions to each question booklet, underline any key words or phrases, such as *least, best, outline, describe*

and the like. In this way you will tend to answer as requested rather than discover on reviewing your paper that you *listed without describing*, that you selected the *worst* choice rather than the *best* choice, etc.

3) If the examination is of the objective or multiple-choice type – that is, each question will also give a series of possible answers: A, B, C or D, and you are called upon to select the best answer and write the letter next to that answer on your answer paper – it is advisable to start answering each question in turn. There may be anywhere from 50 to 100 such questions in the three or four hours allotted and you can see how much time would be taken if you read through all the questions before beginning to answer any. Furthermore, if you come across a question or group of questions which you know would be difficult to answer, it would undoubtedly affect your handling of all the other questions.

4) If the examination is of the essay type and contains but a few questions, it is a moot point as to whether you should read all the questions before starting to answer any one. Of course, if you are given a choice – say five out of seven and the like – then it is essential to read all the questions so you can eliminate the two that are most difficult. If, however, you are asked to answer all the questions, there may be danger in trying to answer the easiest one first because you may find that you will spend too much time on it. The best technique is to answer the first question, then proceed to the second, etc.

5) Time your answers. Before the exam begins, write down the time it started, then add the time allowed for the examination and write down the time it must be completed, then divide the time available somewhat as follows:
   - If 3-1/2 hours are allowed, that would be 210 minutes. If you have 80 objective-type questions, that would be an average of 2-1/2 minutes per question. Allow yourself no more than 2 minutes per question, or a total of 160 minutes, which will permit about 50 minutes to review.
   - If for the time allotment of 210 minutes there are 7 essay questions to answer, that would average about 30 minutes a question. Give yourself only 25 minutes per question so that you have about 35 minutes to review.

6) The most important instruction is to *read each question* and make sure you know what is wanted. The second most important instruction is to *time yourself properly* so that you answer every question. The third most important instruction is to *answer every question*. Guess if you have to but include something for each question. Remember that you will receive no credit for a blank and will probably receive some credit if you write something in answer to an essay question. If you guess a letter – say "B" for a multiple-choice question – you may have guessed right. If you leave a blank as an answer to a multiple-choice question, the examiners may respect your feelings but it will not add a point to your score. Some exams may penalize you for wrong answers, so in such cases *only*, you may not want to guess unless you have some basis for your answer.

7) Suggestions
    a. Objective-type questions
        1. Examine the question booklet for proper sequence of pages and questions
        2. Read all instructions carefully
        3. Skip any question which seems too difficult; return to it after all other questions have been answered
        4. Apportion your time properly; do not spend too much time on any single question or group of questions
        5. Note and underline key words – *all, most, fewest, least, best, worst, same, opposite,* etc.
        6. Pay particular attention to negatives
        7. Note unusual option, e.g., unduly long, short, complex, different or similar in content to the body of the question
        8. Observe the use of "hedging" words – *probably, may, most likely,* etc.
        9. Make sure that your answer is put next to the same number as the question
        10. Do not second-guess unless you have good reason to believe the second answer is definitely more correct
        11. Cross out original answer if you decide another answer is more accurate; do not erase until you are ready to hand your paper in
        12. Answer all questions; guess unless instructed otherwise
        13. Leave time for review

    b. Essay questions
        1. Read each question carefully
        2. Determine exactly what is wanted. Underline key words or phrases.
        3. Decide on outline or paragraph answer
        4. Include many different points and elements unless asked to develop any one or two points or elements
        5. Show impartiality by giving pros and cons unless directed to select one side only
        6. Make and write down any assumptions you find necessary to answer the questions
        7. Watch your English, grammar, punctuation and choice of words
        8. Time your answers; don't crowd material

8) Answering the essay question

Most essay questions can be answered by framing the specific response around several key words or ideas. Here are a few such key words or ideas:

M's: manpower, materials, methods, money, management
P's: purpose, program, policy, plan, procedure, practice, problems, pitfalls, personnel, public relations
a. Six basic steps in handling problems:
    1. Preliminary plan and background development
    2. Collect information, data and facts
    3. Analyze and interpret information, data and facts
    4. Analyze and develop solutions as well as make recommendations

5. Prepare report and sell recommendations
6. Install recommendations and follow up effectiveness

b. Pitfalls to avoid
1. *Taking things for granted* – A statement of the situation does not necessarily imply that each of the elements is necessarily true; for example, a complaint may be invalid and biased so that all that can be taken for granted is that a complaint has been registered
2. *Considering only one side of a situation* – Wherever possible, indicate several alternatives and then point out the reasons you selected the best one
3. *Failing to indicate follow up* – Whenever your answer indicates action on your part, make certain that you will take proper follow-up action to see how successful your recommendations, procedures or actions turn out to be
4. *Taking too long in answering any single question* – Remember to time your answers properly

EXAMINATION SECTION

INTERPRETATION OF LITERARY MATERIALS

INTRODUCTION

The basis of this test lies in the comprehension and interpretation of selected passages, which may be prose or verse, and have been culled from American and English literature, classical and modern. The examinee then answers a series of multiple-choice questions of the four-item type relating to the selection. About one-third of the passages are poetry, and two-thirds are prose.

The following standards of literary interpretation form the major criteria of this test:

1. The ability to understand the literal and figurative meanings of words as used in the passage

2. The ability to glean facts and to grasp the main thought or theme

3. The ability to discern or to relate the purpose, the mood or tone, or the point of view of the passage or of its author

4. The ability to detect and to assess the use of simple literary techniques.

The candidate should note that this is a test of reading comprehension and that the answers for the most part are to be found in and by and through the text. Only a small portion of the questions is involved with or depends upon acquired basal or related information or knowledge.

The *Tests* that follow have been planned to include, or to evolve, in equivalent form, quality, and degree of difficulty, all of the aims set forth above for this sector. The passages have been selected and presented, so far as possible, in ascending order of difficulty to achieve optimum self-instructional progression and maximum learning affect.

To achieve these purposes, fifteen (15) *Tests* are so offered, with answers, and with the answers fully explained, so that the candidate may learn how to go about answering the questions as well as the bases involved in attaining to the correct answers. The book thus becomes a complete self-instructional programmed vehicle.

In addition, as a follow-up and as a reservoir for practice and drill and work-study, fifteen (15) additional passages appear, in a similar gradation of difficulty and with an equal consistency. The correct answers are furnished for these questions.

Note: The questions in the *Tests* are presented for the most part in a five-item-choice form, which means that these questions are approximately 20% more difficult than the ones to be encountered on the Examination. This presentation should result in more extended effort and help to eliminate more surely any reliance on the element of guessing, or any resignation into a mood of indifference to preparation.

Note: Poetry, as well as prose, furnishes the text of some of the passages. To those candidates who, for undefinable reasons, regard the poetry passage as more difficult or less comprehensible than the prose selection, this assurance is offered: It is not so. Both types of passages are equally difficult and equally comprehensible. For this reason, poetry selections appear herein and the answers are given, together with full explanations therefor.

The directions for Test - INTERPRETATION OF LITERARY MATERIALS are approximately as follows, and these directions will govern the *Tests* that follow.

DIRECTIONS: You have two hours for this test. As you answer the questions, you should omit any that seem unusually difficult until you finish the others.

Your answers to the exercises in this test are to be recorded on the separate answer sheet, which is loosely inserted in the test. Remove this answer sheet now; write your name and the other information called for in the blanks at the top of the answer sheet; then finish reading these directions. You may find that these questions will require you to read the selections much more carefully and analytically than you are accustomed to reading such materials, and that you will need to spend more time on many questions than is usually required in objective achievement tests. You may find that the best procedure to follow is to read the selection through once quite carefully; then read all of the questions based on the selection, answering on the first reading as many questions as you can answer easily. Then reread the selection as many times as is necessary the more difficult questions.

After the number on the answer sheet corresponding to that of each exercise, mark the ONE numbered space which designates the answer you have selected as correct.

Sample question and answers follow.

SAMPLE QUESTIONS

DIRECTIONS: In the passage that follows, each question or incomplete statement below is followed by several suggested answers or completions. Select the one that BEST answers the question or completes the statement. Base your choice in each case on the materials given and on your own understanding of the subject matter.

PASSAGE

Tiger, tiger, burning bright
In the forests of the night,
What immortal hand or eye
Could frame thy fearful symmetry?

1. The meter of the poem is

    A. iambic   B. anapestic   C. trochaic
    D. dactylic   E. spondaic

1.___

Item C is correct. The trochee consists of two syllables: one accented, followed by one unaccented. The other items, A, B, D, and E, present different combinations of accented and unaccented syllables.

An IAMB (Item A) is a metrical foot of two syllables, a short followed by a long, or an unaccented by an accented (U -), as in *Come live/with me/and be/my love*.

An ANAPEST (Item B) is a metrical foot of three syllables: two short followed by one long (quantitative meter), or two unstressed followed by one stressed (accentual meter). Thus, *for the nonce* is an accentual anapest.

A TROCHEE (Item C) is a metrical foot of two syllables: a long followed by a short, or an accented followed by an unaccented.

A DACTYL (Item D) is a metrical foot of three syllables: one long followed by two short, or, in modern verse, one accented followed by two unaccented $(-\cup\cup)$, as in *Géntly and hūmănly*.

A SPONDEE (Item E) is a metrical foot consisting of two long syllables or two heavy beats.

2. The words *Tiger, tiger* and the words *burning bright* represent

    A. allusion   B. couplet   C. antithesis
    D. simile   E. alliteration

Item E is correct. Alliteration is the commencement of two or more words of a word group with the same consonant or letter, for the purpose of effect. Item B represents successive rhyming lines. Item C is the contrasting of one idea against another. Item A is a form of reference. Item D is an expressed comparison.

3. The question asked in the poem is:

    A. Who could hold the tiger?
    B. Who could paint such a thing as a tiger?
    C. Who made the tiger?
    D. Who would dare go near a tiger?
    E. Who could describe a tiger?

Item C is correct. The word *frame* in the poem, in this case, means to fashion or mold. Items A, B, D, and E are incorrect.

4. The above lines of the poem represent a(n)

    A. ode   B. oxymoron   C. ottava rima
    D. sestet   E. quatrain

Item E is correct. A four-line stanza is termed a quatrain. Items A, B, C, and D are false.

An ODE (Item A) is a lyric poem, typically of elaborate or irregular metrical form and expressive of exalted or enthusiastic emotion.

OXYMORON is a rhetorical figure of speech by which a locution produces an effect by a seeming self-contradiction, as in *cruel kindness* or *to make haste slowly*.

OTTAVA RIMA, in prosody, is an Italian stanza of eight lines, each of eleven syllables (or, in the English adaptation, of ten or eleven syllables), the first six lines riming alternately and the last two forming a couplet with a different rime (used in Keats' ISABELLA and Byron's DON JUAN).

SESTET is the last six lines of a sonnet.

QUATRAIN is a stanza or poem of four lines, usually with alternate rhymes.

5. This famous poem was written by 5.___

   A. Samuel Taylor
   B. Alexander Pope
   C. Alfred Tennyson
   D. William Blake
   E. John Milton

   William Blake wrote this poem. Therefore, item D is correct. Items A, B, C, and E are false.

6. Blake also wrote 6.___

   A. SONGS OF INNOCENCE
   B. ELEGY WRITTEN IN A COUNTRY CHURCHYARD
   C. TO ALTHEA FROM PRISON
   D. LYCIDAS
   E. PARADISE LOST

   Item A was written by Blake. Item B by Thomas Gray; Item C by Richard Lovelace; Item D by Milton; Item E by Milton.

INTERPRETATION OF LITERARY MATERIALS

EXAMINATION SECTION
TEST 1

PASSAGE

Once he was established as a playwright with MAN AND SUPERMAN in 1905, he settled down to a swift, assertive prose style that was brilliant and unique, in plays as well as prefaces. He did not play tricks with the language. The sentence structure was not varied much, nor was the tension relieved by rhetoric. Shaw was solely concerned with communicating the energy of his mind.

He composed the preface to PYGMALION in Pitman shorthand, which his secretary then transcribed. That indicates the speed with which he wrote, and perhaps also accounts for the leanness of the style. He did not waste time on literary flourishes. Nothing was important except the idea. For ideas were his obsession. He took voluptuous pleasure in them. To him they were things, and he lived among them as most men wallow in creature comforts.

Ascetic and puritanical, he had no taste for any kind of debauches except intellectual arguments. BACK TO METHUSELAH, 418 pages long, was his most reckless orgy. A METABIOLOGICAL PENTATEUCH he called the play, thereby alienating both the reader and the playgoer. Although the play was produced by the Theatre Guild in 1922 and by Barry Jackson at the Birmingham Repertory Theatre, Shaw knew that it could never be popular with audiences, as MAN AND SUPERMAN had been. But as the foremost literary intellectual of his time, he could not refrain from making a Jovian statement about the human race-which was the preoccupation of his lifetime.

QUESTIONS

1. The author feels that Shaw's play BACK TO METHUSELAH, which he calls A METABIOLOGICAL PENTATEUCH, would alienate the reader and playgoer because

    A. it sounds too complex and confusing
    B. it would not appeal to the intellectual
    C. they would probably find it overlong and tedious
    D. it is obviously dated
    E. audiences prefer musicals to dramas

2. Shaw sometimes used shorthand because

    A. he used to be a secretary
    B. it enabled him to use literary flourishes quickly
    C. his style would then become lean and taut
    D. it was more suited to the speed of his thoughts
    E. it enabled him to sufficiently embellish his ideas

3. The play that was to establish Shaw as a playwright was

A. ST. JOAN
C. MAN AND SUPERMAN
E. MAJOR BARBARA
B. DON JUAN IN HELL
D. PYGMALION

4. Characteristics of Shaw, the playwright, and, probably, qualities of Shaw, the man, were

   A. ribald wit and scorn
   B. gregariousness and humor
   C. recklessness and belligerence
   D. mysticism and asceticism
   E. asceticism and puritanism

5. His prose style, if one were limited to one word, might BEST be described as

   A. assertive   B. biting   C. voluptuous
   D. intense   E. polished

6. *Shavian* is a

   A. word invented by Shaw
   B. word reserved exclusively for Shaw, the man and his works
   C. word applied to anything resembling the thought and humor of George Bernard Shaw
   D. word for works belonging to the period in which George Bernard Shaw lived and wrote
   E. derogatory term for Shaw's works

7. Two well-known works by Shaw are _____ and _____.

   A. ANTONY AND CLEOPATRA; SONNETS
   B. THE DAY OF THE RABBLEMENT; POMES PENYEACH
   C. CAESAR AND CLEOPATRA; ANDROCLES AND THE LION
   D. SAILOR OFF THE BREMAN; WELCOME TO THE CITY
   E. THE PLOUGH AND THE STARS; THE SILVER TASSIE

KEY (CORRECT ANSWERS)

1. C
2. D
3. C
4. E
5. A
6. C
7. C

EXPLANATION OF ANSWERS

1. From the title and sub-title, the reader finds that the play deals with the first five books of the Old Testament (Pentateuch), transcends biology (metabiological), and dates back to the time of Methuselah. C is the correct answer.

2. In the passage, the author states that Shaw was not fond of flourishes or embellishments. This eliminates B and E. C is incorrect because his style would not be influenced by his method. Therefore, D must be the correct answer, particularly in view of the second sentence in the second paragraph, viz., *That indicates the speed with which he wrote....*

3. The correct answer is stated in the first sentence of the passage where the author writes, *Once he was established as a playwright with MAN AND SUPERMAN in 1905...* C is the correct answer.

4. The first sentence of paragraph 3 terms Shaw *ascetic and puritanical.* Though he possessed great humor and wit, they did not exist alongside the other qualities stated here. E is the correct answer.

5. In sentence 1, the author states that *...he settled down to a swift, assertive prose style that was brilliant and unique....* A is the correct answer. C and E are obviously not suited to Shaw. B and D are not mentioned in the passage.

6. *Shavian* is not another word for Shaw; the man, his works, nor his period. It is, rather, a term for that which resembles his thought. C is the correct answer.

7. Of the above, A lists the works of Shakespeare; B, James Joyce; C, G.B. Shaw; D, Irwin Shaw; and 5, Sean O'Casey. C is the correct answer.

TEST 2
PASSAGE

One day, a few years ago, during a lunch table discussion about eroticism and sin, Andre Malraux suddenly asked Andre Gide for his definition of a Christian. Gide, who had been visibly dazzled by Malraux' torrential discourse-he has a habit of illustrating such discourses by carrying on a kind of aerial dogfight with a smoking cigarette-hesitated a moment and then remarked, with that quiet verbal hand-wringing which was so peculiarly his: "I feel I am going to be flunked again."

Things have changed a good deal since then. If Gide were alive today, it would be easy enough for him to turn the tables on his former examiner by awarding Malraux a D-or, at best, an inglorious C-plus-for his stewardship as Minister of Cultural Affairs.

Let us be fair to Malraux. No man in France, with the possible exception of Charles de Gaulle, has been more a victim of his own myth. The French, ever since Joan of Arc, have tended to believe in miracles, and Malraux is only the latest in a long series of heroes who seemed ideally suited to fill the bill. If France's culture was imperiled by bureaucratic paralysis, bourgeois complacency or public apathy, then what man was better fitted to play the role of providential savior than the revolutionary author of MAN'S HOPE, the romantic Man of Destiny with the pale Napoleonic brow?

So thought the enthusiasts when Malraux took the job three years ago. Malraux, the orientalist who set out for the Far East when he was 22 and worked his way through the Cambodian jungle to uncover the half-buried temple ruins of Bantai Frey; Malraux, the precocious author of half a dozen novels who won France's highest literary award, the Prix Goncourt, when he was barely 32 (for MAN'S FATE, published in 1933); Malraux, the impassioned archaeologist who ...

QUESTIONS

1. Gide probably did NOT supply Malraux with the requested definition because

   A. he did not believe Malraux wanted an answer
   B. he did not expect Malraux would agree
   C. the question was of too personal a nature
   D. he felt somewhat intimidated by Malraux's discourse
   E. he felt Malraux was far more brilliant than he

2. As Minister of Cultural Affairs, Malraux

   A. fulfilled the expectations of the people of France
   B. is second only to De Gaulle in popularity and success
   C. might be considered a near-failure
   D. has worked a small miracle
   E. is an abysmal failure

3. The author of MAN'S HOPE was

   A. De Gaulle
   B. Andre Gide
   C. Bantai Frey
   D. Joan of Arc
   E. Andre Malraux

4. After listing Malraux's accomplishments, the author is apparently about to go on to say that

   A. this man had to be successful in any undertaking
   B. Malraux was probably over-qualified for the job of Minister of Cultural Affairs
   C. his greatest achievement was in politically serving France
   D. a man with so many interests and accomplishments could not possibly excel in politics
   E. Malraux, unexpectedly, failed to do well as Minister of Cultural Affairs

5. Two well-known works of Malraux are _____ and _____.

   A. ARIEL, a biography of Shelley; THE SILENCE OF COLONEL BRAMBLE
   B. THE ROYAL WAY; MAN'S FATE
   C. OEDIPE; LA PUCELLE D'ORLEANS
   D. GARGANTUA; PANTAGUEL
   E. THE MAIDS; THE BLACKS

6. A famous work of Andre Gide's is

   A. SYMPHONY PASTORAL
   B. OUR LADY OF THE FLOWERS
   C. WAITING FOR GODOT
   D. THE TIME OF YOUR LIFE
   E. CALIGULA

KEY (CORRECT ANSWERS)

1. D   4. E
2. C   5. B
3. E   6. A

EXPLANATION OF ANSWERS

1. There is no basis for answers A and B. Answer E is not implied in the passage. C is, of course, false. D, however, while not directly stated, is indicated in sentence 3 of paragraph 1 and in the last sentence of paragraph 1.

2. According to the passage, the people of France did expect much from Malraux; therefore, answers A, B, and D are incorrect. The correct answer, C, is indicated in sentence 2, paragraph 2. Answer E is incorrect because it expresses too harsh a judgment.

3. At the end of the passage, it is mentioned that Malraux won the Prix Goncourt for MAN'S HOPE. Therefore, the proper answer is E.

4. From the opening sentence of paragraph 4, one gathers that the author is about to go on to prove the *enthusiasts* wrong. Therefore, E is the correct answer. D is incorrect because it is in no way to be inferred that Malraux's previous accomplishments and a political career would be incompatible; in fact, the opposite is to be deduced.

5. Of the listed items, A lists two works of Andre Maurois; B, Andre Malraux; C, Voltaire; D, Rabelais; and E, Jean Genet. Therefore, B is the correct answer.

6. A is the work of Andre Gide, the correct answer; B of Genet; C of Beckett; D of Saroyan; E of Camus.

TEST 3

PASSAGE

In deciding to send the heir to the throne to Gordonstoun, about the least conventional public school in Britain, the Queen has initiated a new pattern of princely education. For Gordonstoun is significantly different from the socially exclusive kind of public school, like Eton or Harrow, which English princes might naturally be expected to attend.

Oddly enough, this has very little to do with its educational system, or with the fact that it was founded by a German, Kurt Hahn, who was expelled by the Nazis. Indeed, as far as education goes, Gordonstoun is probably far more like the Rugby of Tom Brown's school days than Rugby itself is now, and Dr. Hahn, who even in Germany was fascinated by British public school methods and by the ideals which inspired them, has probably much more in common with the nineteenth century Dr. Arnold than have most British headmasters of today.

Why, then, is the decision to send 13-year-old Prince Charles to Gordonstoun, starting with the summer term May 1, so remarkable? The answer, of course, is that what really distinguishes the top-rank British public school is not its type of education but the class of boy who goes there. What is unique about Eton is not the way it teaches Latin or math, but the fact that virtually all its pupils come either from the upper class or upper middle class.

In other words, the essence of Eton is not educational but social. Thus the significance of the decision not to send Prince Charles there, and not to have him educated by private tutors, but to send him instead to Gordonstoun, is not that he will get an education radically different from that of his predecessors, but that he will be the first monarch to be educated in an institution which is fundamentally classless.

QUESTIONS

1. In the passage, the *heir to the throne* is referred to.
   This specifically means

   A. the children of the Royal Family
   B. the son of the Queen
   C. the children of Queen Elizabeth
   D. Prince Andrew
   E. Prince Charles

2. Gordonstoun is a significantly different school because

   A. it is progressive
   B. one might expect an English prince to attend it
   C. it is essentially social rather than educational
   D. it is fundamentally classless
   E. it was founded by a German

3. It would seem to be the Queen's wish that

   A. her son receive a progressive education
   B. Prince Charles be educated by private tutors
   C. her son follow in his predecessors' footsteps
   D. England shall become a classless society

E. the Prince shall be educated quite differently than his predecessors

4. Dr. Hahn, the passage implies, had something in common with

    A. German education   B. the Nazis
    C. Dr. Arnold   D. British headmasters
    E. the 19th century

5. The relationship of Prince Charles to the late King George is that of

    A. grandfather   B. nephew   C. son
    D. grandson   E. father

6. The Duke of Edinburgh is

    A. the husband of Princess Margaret
    B. the husband of Queen Elizabeth
    C. a cousin of Prince Charles
    D. the King of England
    E. the brother of Queen Elizabeth

KEY (CORRECT ANSWERS)

1.	E	4.	C
2.	D	5.	D
3.	E	6.	B

EXPLANATION OF ANSWERS

1. The passage is about the older son of Queen Elizabeth, Prince Charles, who is heir to the throne. He is mentioned in sentence 1, paragraph 3. E is the correct answer.

2. The last sentence of the passage states that the school is fundamentally classless. E is the only other true statement about the school but it is not a significant difference. D is the correct answer.

3. One may surmise from the passage that the Queen's wish is E. It is stated that the school does not provide a progressive education, which discounts A. B and C, it is stated, are what the Queen does not want. D is neither mentioned nor implied. The correct answer is E.

4. The correct answer is C. He had, as stated in the passage, nothing in common with A and B; little, it is implied, with D. And his name was linked with *nineteenth century Dr. Arnold's,* not with the nineteenth century.

5. Prince Charles is the son of Queen Elizabeth. She is the daughter of the late King George. Therefore, D is the correct answer.

6. The Duke of Edinburgh is the husband of Queen Elizabeth and the father of Prince Charles. B is the correct answer.

TEST 4

PASSAGE

But how can I say if we'll get by again? I don't know enough of the details of how the bombs work, how things are going. It's a three-way race. There's the long race to develop our culture. The whole story of thousands of years, Greece, Palestine, Magna Charta, the French Revolution, it's the story of a boy growing up, learning to straighten his shoulders. But we haven't learned enough yet to live side by side. Then there is technology, the excesses of scientists who learn how to make things much faster than we can learn what to do with them. The third runner is the strain between two parts of the world that grew up unevenly.

You know, the Russians have banned my work. They banned OUR TOWN (a drama of the beauty of everyday joys and cares) because they were campaigning against the family at the time and it is a family story. And they banned THE SKIN OF OUR TEETH because they said it equated war with flood and the ice age as natural catastrophes, when every good Marxist knows war is only the work of capitalists. Wars and human disasters come from the ugly unresolved things in us, just as earthquakes come from ugly unresolved things in nature, the cooling of the earth's crust.

I have no patience with people who say they love nature and go out to look at a field on Sunday afternoon. Our families, the way we live with our fellowmen, are a part of nature, too.

QUESTIONS

1. The speaker in the passage makes a comparison between

    A. the development of the culture of the human race and a boy growing up
    B. two parts of the world
    C. technology and the scientists
    D. Russia and the U.S.
    E. the Magna Charta and the French Revolution

2. The Russians banned THE SKIN OF OUR TEETH because they felt

    A. wars come from the unresolved things in human beings
    B. it contained the same sort of message as OUR TOWN
    C. it spoke of floods and the ice age as natural catastrophes
    D. it considered war a natural catastrophe
    E. the playwright was a capitalist

3. The speaker has no patience with those who

    A. think of nature as something to look at
    B. believe that wars are inevitable
    C. profess to love people and nature
    D. think nature is more important than how we live with our fellowmen
    E. say they love nature and do nothing about it

4. The speaker feels that wars

A. are the work of Marxists
B. are the work of unresolved inner human conflict
C. are the work of capitalists
D. will continue as long as the scientists continue to learn how to make things faster than we can learn what to do with them
E. though bound to reoccur, will always be survived

5. The man who is speaking his thoughts in the passage is 5.____

   A. Maxwell Anderson   B. Elmer Rice
   C. William Saroyan   D. Thornton Wilder
   E. Tennessee Williams

6. Aside from being a playwright, he is also a novelist. One of his novels is 6.____

   A. THE BRIDGE OF SAN LUIS REY
   B. THE GRAPES OF WRATH
   C. MISS LONELYHEARTS
   D. THE DAY OF THE LOCUST
   E. THE LOVED ONE

KEY (CORRECT ANSWERS)

1. A 4. B
2. D 5. D
3. A 6. A

EXPLANATIONS OF ANSWERS

1. In paragraph 1, the speaker states, *There's the long race to develop our culture.... it 's the story of a boy growing up....* The correct answer, then, is A. Though the other answers are mentioned in the passage, no comparisons are drawn.

2. The answer is contained in paragraph 2, where the speaker states, *they said it equated ... and the ice age as natural catastrophes.* D is the correct answer. C and E ... and A is the sentiment of the playwright, not the Russians.

3. ... how we live with our fellowmen is nature too. This is explained in ... answer is A and can be found in the first sentence of the last ...

4. ... *unresolved things in us,* the speaker says in paragraph 2. ... answer. A and D are neither stated nor implied. C is said sar... e first sentence of the passage.

5. ... OF OUR TEETH, and winner of the Pulitzer Prize for OUR ... ilder. Therefore, D is correct.

6. Of the ... ns, A is correct since it is the work of Thornton Wilder; B is the work of John Steinbeck; C, of Nathaniel West; D, of Nathaniel West; E, of Evelyn Waugh.

TEST 5

PASSAGE

Improvisation of sketches, whether topical or not, is a chancy affair. It goes best when practiced, like a parlor game, among friends. There is more risk in a cafe or night club, but with relaxed, imbibing customers around the performers, it takes on the atmosphere of communal sport. In a theater with a sober, paying audience waiting in expectant rows to be entertained swiftly and efficiently, improvisation is all but impossible.

Indeed, sketches that bear the birthmarks of improvisatory genesis seldom hold up in the formal procedures of a theater revue. They have a tendency to stammer and dawdle, to seem coy and amateurish. They make an audience restless, for they spread a sense of indecision and ineffectualness, and there is little that is more disaffecting in the theater than a lack of authority and control on the stage.

All the revues bred in improvisation that have tackled Broadway in recent years have had moments when they fell into doldrums, as if the performers were praying for any kind of a wind. One does not speak of a passing lapse of memory or a miscue, which could happen on any stage in any performance, but of doubts and hesitant attacks left over from the improvisatory embryo.

QUESTIONS

1. The writer seems to feel that improvisations

    A. are a vital embryo from which spontaneous ideas evolve
    B. hold up well under the formal procedures of a revue
    C. do not really belong in the theatre
    D. are a swift and efficient entertainment
    E. are best executed in the nightclub or cafe

2. An improvisation is a risky thing because

    A. performers often miss their cue
    B. it leads to a sense of indecision and ineffectualness
    C. performers are fraught with lapses of memory
    D. it can unsettle an audience by the lack of authority and control on the stage
    E. since much is not committed to memory, there can occur silences where the performers lose their direction

3. The theme of the passage seems to be that

    A. improvisation should be stricken and abolished from the theatre
    B. improvisation is a vital tool but should be reserved for the actors' schools
    C. improvisations are a frail reed on which to depend in the theatre
    D. only the most skilled can successfully employ improvisation to the point where it becomes theatre
    E. only the most successful improvisation can affect the audience as would the well-written speech of a good playwright

4. The writer of *sketches that bear the birthmarks of improvisatory genesis.* By this, he means

A. otherwise well-prepared sketches that seem to flounder midway
B. sketches that have been badly written by a lesser playwright
C. sketches that obviously began as improvisations
D. an improvisation that is all too obviously made up as the actor proceeds
E. a rich nature will improvise more rewardingly than an indigent one

5. An example of improvisation in the theatre would be

    A. the presentations of the ACTORS' STUDIO
    B. any ad lib or aside supplied by the actor rather than the playwright
    C. the sketches of Nichols and May
    D. the sketches of a Noel Coward revue
    E. any dialogue where performers do not adhere faithfully to their words as written

6. The remarks might appear as or in

    A. a book review
    B. a drama review
    C. WHO'S WHO IN THE THEATRE
    D. the preface to a play
    E. the news section of any newspaper

KEY (CORRECT ANSWERS)

1. C
2. D
3. C
4. C
5. C
6. B

EXPLANATION OF ANSWERS

1. Answers B and D, the author most definitely does not believe. A is not stated. And the author feels they go best when ...*practiced among friends,* which discounts E. Though he uses other words, the author does seem to be of the opinion of item C, which is the correct answer.

2. The correct answer is D. E does occur in improvisation, but that is not what makes it risky. B is often the result but not the aim. C and E are invalid for the same reason. A is false because there are no cues in improvisation.

3. The author's ever-recurring theme would be item C. Nowhere are answers B, D, or E stated or implied. Answer A is a harsher statement than the author makes, and so is false.

4. The correct answer is C. By the term *improvisitory genesis,* the author is referring to that which begins as improvisation. None of the other items is mentioned in the passage.

5. C is the correct answer. Noel Coward as a playwright does not use improvisational techniques; this discounts item D. The Actors' Studio do not use improvisation in their presentation of plays, but only in their classrooms. This discounts answer A. B and E do not constitute a definition of improvisation.

6. The correct answer is B. None of the other answers is suited to the material or the type of presentation used in the passage.

TEST 6

PASSAGE

BURNT NORTON

*Time present and time past
Are both perhaps present in time future,
And time future contained in time past.
If all time is eternally present
All time is unredeemable.
What might have been is an abstraction
Remaining a perpetual possibility
Only in a world of speculation.
What might have been and what has been
Point to one end, which is always present.
Footfalls echo in the memory
Down the passage which we did not take
Towards the door we never opened
Into the rose-garden. My words echo
Thus, in your mind.
                   But to what purpose
Disturbing the dust on a bowl of rose-leaves
I do not know.*

QUESTIONS

1. The essential point concerning time that the poet is trying to make is:

    A. Time is an abstraction
    B. Past time is contained in future time
    C. It is eternally present
    D. Present time is contained in past time
    E. That it exists in a world of speculation

2. There is a relationship in the poem between *What might have been* and

    A. ... one end, which is always present
    B. ... memory
    C. ... The passage which we took
    D. ... the door we never opened
    E. ... a bowl of rose-leaves

3. The rose-garden is meant to symbolize

    A. past happiness experiences
    B. Nirvana
    C. Heaven
    D. life after death
    E. something unattained

4. The poem was written by the author of THE WASTE LAND, an expatriate American; he is

A. Lawrence Durrell B. Thomas Stearns Eliot C. Ezra Pound
D. Allen Ginsberg E. Robert Frost

5. Of the following, this poet did NOT write 5.____

   A. THE FAMILY REUNION
   B. THE UNVANQUISHED
   C. FOUR QUARTETTES
   D. OLD POSSUM'S BOOK OF PRACTICAL CATS
   E. MURDER IN THE CATHEDRAL

6. Probably his MOST famous character is 6.____

   A. Miniver Cheevy B. Ichabod Crane
   C. Thomas a Becket D. Alfred J. Prufrock
   E. Mrs. Erlynne

KEY (CORRECT ANSWERS)

1. C   4. B
2. D   5. B
3. E   6. D

EXPLANATION OF ANSWERS

1. In reading the poem, the reader is presented with the hypothesis in line 4 from which all the other conclusions about time are formed. Item C, then, is the correct answer.

2. The closest in meaning would be D. There is no other choice presented that relates to the line, *What might have been....*

3. The poet says, *Footfalls echo in the memory... towards the door we never opened into the rose-garden.* He is speaking of a human condition. E, then, is the correct answer. B, C, and D have nothing to do with memory.

4. Eliot, item B, is the correct answer, and THE WASTE LAND is his most famous work.

5. The only work not written by Eliot is item B, which was written by William Faulkner.

6. Prufrock, item D, is distinctly Eliot's. He exists in THE LOVE SONG OF ALFRED J. PRUFROCK, as the passive New Englander who lives a life without meaning.

TEST 7

PASSAGE

I want to make a few admissions and disclosures. My poems on Hawthorne and Edwards draw heavily on prose sentences by their subjects. THE SCREAM owes everything to Elizabeth Bishop's beautiful, calm story, IN THE VILLAGE. THE LESSON picks up a phrase or two from Rafael Alberti. RETURNING was suggested by Giuseppe Ungaretti's CANZONE. THE PUBLIC GARDEN is a recasting and clarification of an old confusing poem of mine called DAVID AND BATHSHEBA IN THE PUBLIC GARDEN. BEYOND THE ALPS is the poem I published in LIFE STUDIES, but with a stanza restored at the suggestion of John Berryman.

He has a great gift for friendship. No one is more generous than Robert Lowell in acknowledging his indebtedness to anybody who has ever helped him with a problem or with a poem.

The poets who most directly influenced me, he says, were Allen Tate, Elizabeth Bishop, and William Carlos Williams. An unlikely combination! ... but you can see that Bishop is a sort of bridge between Tate's formalism and Williams' informal art. For sheer language, Williams beats anybody. And who compares with him for aliveness and keenness of observation? I admire Pound but find it impossible to imitate him. Nor do I know how to use Eliot or Auden-their voice is so personal. Williams can be used, partly because he is somewhat anonymous. His poems are as perfect as anybody's, but they lead one to think of the possibility of writing them in different ways-for example, putting them into rhyme.

QUESTIONS

1. The poem DAVID AND BATHSHEBA IN THE PUBLIC GARDEN referred to in the passage was written by

   A. Elizabeth Bishop
   B. Nathaniel Hawthorne
   C. Rafael Alberti
   D. Robert Lowell
   E. Giuseppe Ungaretti

2. In the passage, Elizabeth Bishop is referred to as

   A. the poetess who wrote THE SCREAM
   B. a person with a great gift for friendships
   C. the poet who most greatly influenced Lowell
   D. incomparable for aliveness and keenness of observation
   E. a bridge between Tate and Williams

3. One gets the impression from the passage that Lowell

   A. can hardly be considered an original poet because he borrowed so liberally from so many sources
   B. feels a great debt to such poets as Pound and Eliot
   C. is indebted to many poets and readily acknowledges this debt
   D. though he speaks highly of certain other poets, considers himself superior as a poet
   E. considers Williams lacking as a poet because his poems do not rhyme

4. The three poets mentioned in the passage by last name only refer to

A. George Eliot, Tennessee Williams, and W.H. Auden
B. Allen Tate, William Carlos Williams, and Elizabeth Bishop
C. Ezra Pound, W.H. Auden, and T.S. Eliot
D. John Berryman, T.S. Eliot, and Nathaniel Hawthorne
E. Rafael Alberti, Ezra Pound, and T.S. Eliot

5. Some of the works written by William Carlos Williams, though not mentioned in the passage, are

    A. ADAM AND EVE AND THE CITY, AN EARLY MARTYR, and SPRING AND ALL
    B. THE HOLLOW MEN, OLD POSSUM'S BOOK OF PRACTICAL CATS, and FOUR QUARTETS
    C. CANTOS, EXULTATIONS, and RIPOSTES
    D. THE ORATORS, THE DANCE OF DEATH, and THE DOG BENEATH THE SKIN
    E. THE CRITIQUE OF HUMANISM, MR. POPE, and THE MEDITERRANEAN

6. The passage might be considered illustrative of a part of the kind of article that might be found in

    A. an Art news periodical
    B. THE READER'S ENCYCLOPEDIA
    C. THE WORLD ALMANAC
    D. THE TIMES BOOK REVIEW (or A WRITERS' DIGEST)
    E. TIME magazine's literary section

KEY (CORRECT ANSWERS)

1. D   4. C
2. E   5. A
3. C   6. D

EXPLANATION OF ANSWERS

1. Toward the end of paragraph 1, the title is mentioned as *an old ....poem of mine*. In paragraph 2, the speaker is revealed to be Robert Lowell. All the poets mentioned in paragraph 1 are listed in relation to the poems they wrote; however, the above poem was written by Lowell himself. Therefore, the correct answer is D.

2. Only items C and E refer to Elizabeth Bishop. C, however, is inaccurate because she is referred to as one of three poets who most greatly influenced Lowell, all of seemingly equal importance. E, then, is the correct answer.

3. The correct answer is C. one does not get the feeling from the passage that borrowing and originality are incompatible, as suggested in A. Pound and Eliot had no direct influence on him, which discounts B. Nowhere does the reader get the feeling that he considers himself superior, nor that Williams should have made his poems rhyme.

4. C is the only possible correct answer. Toward the end of paragraph 3, Lowell states, *I admire Pound....Nor do I know how to use Eliot or Auden. . . .* George Eliot is known as a novelist, not as a poet; and, though Hawthorne is only mentioned by last name, he too was a novelist.

5. Of the above works, B lists the works of T.S. Eliot; C, the works of Pound; D, the works of Auden; and E, the works of Tate. All of them are poets mentioned in the passage. Only item A lists the works of Williams, and is the correct answer.

6. Items B and C would contain nothing so lengthy as the passage, but would offer a brief biographical sketch. Item E would be a review of a work only. Item D, however, could present a conversation with an author such as the above passage and is the correct answer.

TEST 8

PASSAGE

Intended primarily as a showcase for the artists who have been or are associated with Mr. Maeght's art gallery-Braque, Chagall, Miro, Giacometti-the museum has a separate room for the works of each, and there are additional rooms for other members of Mr. Maeght's stable - among them, Leger, Bazaine, Ubac, Tal Coat.

These rooms are a painter's dream for showing off art. The walls are white, and the paintings are hung not by nails but by suction. The light is ideal-cool and even, illuminating the canvases at the perfect angle of 45 degrees on every day of the year but four. The architect, Mr. Sert, has exiled reflections, the bane of all painting, by banning windows and lighting the rooms by what he calls "light traps." The blazing rays of the Riviera sun strike the roof and are refracted along the curved surfaces of the concrete veils that compose the ceiling according to angles Sert worked out in a specially built laboratory at Harvard.

The artists themselves have played a major role in the construction and decoration of the museum. Miro designed a series of fantastic creatures of ceramic and cement which wind around the foundation like ivy around a tree trunk. There are mosaics by Chagall, Braque, and Tal Coat, and sculpture in the central courtyard and among the surrounding pines.

QUESTIONS

1. A GOOD title for this passage might be

   A. MR. MAEGHT'S ART GALLERY
   B. THE MUSEUM ON THE RIVIERA
   C. FRENCH ART AND ARCHITECTURE
   D. THE SCIENCE OF LIGHT
   E. THE IMPRESSIONIST PAINTERS

2. Why did Mr. Sert ban windows from the rooms of the museum?

   A. This is not an accurate statement. He did not ban windows, but, rather, exiled reflections.
   B. He wished to light the rooms with *light traps* and exile reflections.
   C. Exiled reflections are the bane of all painting.
   D. Refracted natural light and windows cannot satisfactorily exist in the same enclosure.
   E. He preferred natural light to artificial light.

3. An unusual feature of the museum is the part played by the artists in its decorations; for example, there are

   A. ceramics by Braque
   B. mosaics of fantastic creatures
   C. sculpture by Chagall
   D. mosaics by Giacometti
   E. ceramics by Miro

4. The light is considered ideal because

- A. of the angle of illumination
- B. the canvases are illuminated at the perfect angle of 45 degrees on every day of the year
- C. the walls are white
- D. the walls have curved surfaces
- E. Sert worked out the angles in a specially built laboratory at Harvard

5. Two very prominent painters who lived and worked in the vicinity of the museum, but who are not mentioned in the passage, are

- A. Juan Gris and Corot
- B. Manet and Utrillo
- C. Delacroix and Matisse
- D. Picasso and Dubuffet
- E. Seurat and Cezanne

6. The Riviera is

- A. a coastal area bordered by Rapallo and San Remo, on Italy's northern coast
- B. a coastal area extending from Le Havre to Brittany, in the north of France
- C. an island in the Mediterranean, off the coast of Monte Carlo
- D. an area of beaches and small provinces extending from Costa Brava, Spain, to Nice, France
- E. the southern coast of France

KEY (CORRECT ANSWERS)

1. B   4. A
2. B   5. D
3. E   6. E

EXPLANATION OF ANSWERS

1. This passage describes in detail the interior of a museum. Toward the end of paragraph 2, the author mentions ....*the Riviera sun....*, thereby placing it geographically. Items C, D, and E are inappropriate and incorrect. A is directly mentioned in the passage and might be considered were it not for the more inclusive item B, which is the correct answer.

2. B is the correct answer. C and D are false statements. E is not referred to in the passage, and A is incorrect because, in order to exile reflections, he had to ban windows.

3. E is the only possible correct answer. The mosaics are by Chagall and Braque. There is no mention of who did the sculpture. Miro, however, did design ceramic creatures as decoration.

4. Though all the answers, except B (the passage mentions *every day of the year but four*) are factually true, only A directly states why the light is ideal (sentence 3, paragraph 2).

5. Picasso and Dubuffet lived and worked near the museum.

6. The correct answer is E. The Riviera, or Blue Coast, is situated along the southern coast of France.

TEST 9

PASSAGE

JULES RENARD was a minor writer in a time of extraordinary French flowering. As one of the founders of the powerful periodical, MERCURE DE FRANCE, and an early member of the Goncourt Academy, he had a foot in both the Symbolist and the Naturalist camps, generally considered antithetical. Yet, he was a maverick in his journalism, his plays, his famous tale POIL DE CAROTTE (RED HEAD), and in such novels as L'ECORNIFLEUR (THE SCROUNGER). Perhaps this is why, somewhat eclipsed by younger men like Claudel, Gide, Proust, and Valery, he will live chiefly for his comments on his contemporaries.

Having won a reputation in France in the Nineties for his embittered, rather sour pictures of family life (chiefly drawn from his own bickering parents), Renard enjoyed a revival of interest in 1925, when his JOURNAL was posthumously published. With its thumbnail sketches of such friends and acquaintances as Goncourt, Wilde, Claudel, Toulouse-Lautrec, Sarah Bernhardt, and Pierre Loti, and its acerbic comments on the events and follies of his times, the JOURNAL became a source reference for many literary historians who were now far more interested in his contemporaries than in Renard himself.

QUESTIONS

1. Renard is remembered CHIEFLY for the kind of writing that appeared in

    A. POIL DE GAROTTE
    B. L'ECORNIFLEUR
    C. JOURNAL
    D. his plays
    E. his journalism

2. Renard's writing is considered

    A. a part of the Symbolist group
    B. a part of the Naturalist group
    C. influenced by the MERCURE DE FRANCE
    D. a part of both groups
    E. more important than most of his contemporaries

3. The author seems to consider Claudel

    A. the same sort of writer as was Jules Renard
    B. more in a class with Valery than Proust
    C. a better writer than Renard
    D. a minor writer of his period
    E. as having won his reputation with rather sour pictures of his family life

4. Renard enjoyed a revival of interest

    A. as one of the founders of the MERCURE DE FRANCE
    B. after his death
    C. as an early member of the Goncourt Academy
    D. when he was considered a *maverick* in journalism
    E. with the writing of the notes on his family life

5. The period of French writing of which the author is writing is the _____ century.

- A. late 19th
- B. early 19th
- C. early 20th
- D. 18th
- E. turn of the

6. A work written by Marcel Proust is
   - A. THE NABOB
   - B. KINGS IN EXILE
   - C. REMEMBRANCE OF THINGS PAST
   - D. SAPHO
   - E. MADAME BOVARY

KEY (CORRECT ANSWERS)

1. C   4. B
2. D   5. A
3. C   6. C

EXPLANATION OF ANSWERS

1. The passage states (end of first paragraph) that he ...*will live chiefly for his comments on his contemporaries.* Later, in paragraph 2, the reader is told that his JOURNAL contained thumbnail sketches of his friends and acquaintances. Therefore, C is the correct answer. Items A and B are referred to merely as a famous play and novel. Items D and E are mentioned but not elaborated upon.

2. The correct answer here is D and is to be found in the first paragraph of the passage. Regarding item E, most of his contemporaries came to be more famous than Renard (end of second paragraph). Since, as the passage states in paragraph 1, ... *he had a foot in both the Symbolist and Naturalist camps* ... , items A and B must be disregarded as incorrect. Item C is not mentioned as exerting any literary influence.

3. The author states (paragraph 1) that Renard was ...*somewhat eclipsed by younger men like Claudel.* This would indicate that C is the correct answer. Item D actually refers to Renard. The author puts Valery and Proust in the same class, thus discounting B. Item E refers, again, to Renard.

4. Item E won him his reputation, but the revival of interest in him came with the publication of his JOURNAL. It was published posthumously, so the correct answer is B. Since the revival of interest mentioned in the question-stem and item B (the answer) are directly linked in the passage, items A, C, and D must be discarded.

5. The time of which the author is writing is the time of Proust, Toulouse-Lautrec, and Oscar Wilde. It was the late 19th century. Therefore, the correct answer is A. All the other items listed, B, C, D, and E, are false.

6. Items A, B, and D were written by Daudet. Item E was written by Flaubert. The correct answer is C.

TEST 10

PASSAGE

When he died, Thoreau was not quite 45 years old. His claims to fame were slim. He was well-known, of course, in his hometown as sometime pencil manufacturer, surveyor, handyman- an obviously not unbeloved odd stick who had preferred to put in much of his days, no matter what the wind or weather, walking the woods and fields and who had once even lived alone for a couple of years in a shack over by walden Pond.

Even so admiring - however ambivalent - a friend as Emerson felt that Thoreau had failed of some great promise and had ended up as a mere "captain of a huckleberry party. "

Nevertheless, there it was: WALDEN, the masterwork; it was out in the world, and so was the fiery essay on CIVIL DISOBEDIENCE. Thoreau died, and the work began to grow as did the legend of the man.

The growth was slow and partial. Except for the journal, as Henry Seidel Canby noted, all Thoreau's important writings were in print within three years after his death. Nevertheless, he was antipathetic to both the gilded and the genteel age; his continuing survival for most readers was as a nature writer; only in the less sanguine decades of our time-and with books and essays about him from abroad and many studies here at home - has the whole Thoreau emerged.

Thoreau said he required "of every writer, first or last, a simple and sincere account of his own life." That was the requirement he himself strove to meet. yet one must say Thoreau was not a simple man-or better, he was of a simplicity so colossal as to baffle the usual run of hectic mankind.

When he said, famously, that most men "lead lives of quiet desperation," one has no feeling that he included himself. On the contrary, one feels that this eccentric achieved in living a deep sanity and a deep joy. " I wish to know," he beautifully declared, an entire heaven and an entire earth. And did he not?

QUESTIONS

1. The peak of Thoreau's popularity was reached

    A. when he was 45 years of age
    B. directly after the writing of WALDEN
    C. with his essay CIVIL DISOBEDIENCE
    D. three years after his death
    E. in recent generations

2. His hometown, during his lifetime, revered him as

    A. a famous man
    B. a writer
    C. a man of practical, workaday talents
    D. an unbeloved odd stick
    E. the man who lived in a shack near Walden Pond

3. How do we know that Thoreau was *antipathetic to both the gilded and the genteel age?* Because he

   A. did think much of civility and manners
   B. obviously preferred the life of the woods and fields
   C. also liked the towns and cities of America
   D. distrusted all forms of animal life
   E. disliked people

4. Thoreau was, really,

   A. no more unusual than his fellow townsmen
   B. a respected member of the community
   C. much emulated in his hometown
   D. looked upon as a genius
   E. a man, simple in the extreme

5. His famous remark that men *lead lives of quiet desperation* means that they

   A. live in both *heaven and hell*
   B. live as outcasts of society
   C. are victims of conformity
   D. live in a kind of miserable human condition to which they give little or no voice
   E. live as uncomplaining people; as stoics

6. Another work by Thoreau is

   A. REPRESENTATIVE MEN
   B. ESSAYS ON FRIENDSHIP
   C. ENGLISH TRAITS
   D. SOCIETY AND SOLITUDE
   E. A YANKEE IN CANADA

7. A work by Emerson is

   A. THE CONDUCT OF LIFE
   B. THE GATHERING OF THE FORCES
   C. LEAVES OF GRASS
   D. THE HALF-BREED
   E. DRUM-TAPS

KEY (CORRECT ANSWERS)

1. E   5. D
2. C   6. E
3. B   7. A
4. E

EXPLANATION OF ANSWERS

1. E is the desired answer. He died at 45, discounting item A. WALDEN had to wait quite a time to become famous, discounting B. Item D relates to the printing of his writings. And WALDEN is a far more famous work than CIVIL DISOBEDIENCE, discounting item C.

2. He was considered neither a famous man nor a writer during his lifetime; this discounts items A and B. The answer is given in C (see paragraph one). Item D subtly twists the facts and is incorrect; he was NOT unbeloved. Item E is correct, but this is not that for which he was admired by his town.

3. Immediately following the quotation in paragraph 3, the explanation is given that *his continuing survival for most readers was as a nature writer.* B, then, is the correct answer. Items A and C do not relate to the idea of *antipathetic*. D and E are patently false.

4. He is spoken of (in paragraph 5) as possessing a *simplicity so colossal....*, thereby indicating E as the correct completion of the statement. Items A, B, and C are false. And if he were a genius, his townspeople did not look upon him as such (paragraph 1). Thus, item D may be discounted.

5. Item D is the correct answer. *Quiet desperation* is a term given to a kind of unhappiness which cannot be named or talked about. But this does not mean that item E would do as well: most people are NOT stoics. Whether or not items B and C might produce quiet desperation, that is not the kind of basic, inner unhappiness Thoreau had reference to. And the phrase *quiet desperation* leaves no room for any glimpse of heaven, also discounting item A.

6. Item E is the correct answer. All the other works (items A, B, C, and D) were written by Emerson, who was Thoreau!s greatest literary influence.

7. A was written by Emerson. The others (items B, C, D, and E) were written by Whitman, who was also greatly influenced by Emerson.

TEST 11

PASSAGE

Existentialism, as developed in the past 25 years by the French writer-philosopher Jean-Paul Sartre, holds that a man's life acquires meaning only when he makes his choice on an issue that significantly affects his fellow-men - and acts accordingly.

Last week, Mr. Sartre, now 59, chose not to accept the Nobel Prize for literature. He made his stand clear through, his publishers when unofficial reports that he had been selected by the Swedish Academy of Letters reached Paris Tuesday. And he stuck, by his decision when the Academy announced Thursday that it was awarding him the prize for 1964 in recognition of the " vast influence" of his novels, short stories, and plays, with their " spirit of liberty and quest for truth."

To have accepted this honor and the $53,000 that goes with it, Mr. Sartre explained, would have diminished his life's meaning. "A writer, " he said, "must act only with the means that are his ... the written word"; to add to his pen the influence of an institution "is not fair to the reader.... It is not the same if I sign myself jean-paul Sartre or if I sign Jean-Paul Sartre, Nobel Prize winner."

Or, as he had put it in his latest book, THE WORDS: " ... With empty hands and empty pockets...I have set myself to work to save my whole self..."

The owlish, stocky "pope of existentialism" was the first recipient of the Nobel Prize for literature to turn it down fully and freely. (George Bernard Shaw rejected it in 1925 but reconsidered, donating the money toward the translation of Swedish literature, and Boris Pasternak refused to accept it in 1958, but under obvious Soviet pressure.) A Swedish Academy spokesman commented that if Mr. Sartre does not collect the money, it will go back into the Nobel Prize funds, but the award would stand: "The Academy is guided not by a possible winner's wishes but by the decision of its members."

QUESTIONS

1. Sartre feels that choice necessarily must NOT preclude

   A. free will
   D. truth
   B. Existentialism
   E. action
   C. liberty

2. How would the acceptance of the prize have *diminished his life's meaning?* He

   A. would lose the approval he has gained on his own
   B. would cease to write existentially
   C. would come under the influence of the Academy
   D. would cease to act with and within his work
   E. felt the influence of an institution would redound unfavorably upon his readers

3. Sartre, in turning down the award fully and freely,

   A. is the first to do so
   B. may yet accept the money
   C. incurred the wrath of the Academy

D. joins Pasternak and Shaw
E. was acting under Soviet pressure

4. The Nobel Prize is awarded by a(n) _____ Academy.

   A. French
   B. Swedish
   C. American
   D. international
   E. Swiss

5. Why does Sartre feel that to sign himself Jean-Paul Sartre, Nobel Prize winner, would not be fair to the reader?

   A. He feels the award is a political maneuver.
   B. It would hurt the sales of his works in certain countries.
   C. Because he did not actually accept the prize.
   D. It would influence him (the reader) in a way he does not wish to.
   E. He wishes to remain anonymous for the sake of his work.

6. Existentialism has as its basis the teachings of

   A. Locke
   B. Bentham
   C. Russell
   D. Heidegger
   E. Nietzsche

7. A work of Sartre's is

   A. L'HOMME REVOLTE
   B. LE MYTHE DE SISYPHE
   C. UN CHANT D'AMOUR
   D. NAUSEA
   E. L'ETRANGIER

3 (#11)

KEY (CORRECT ANSWERS)

1. E 5. D
2. D 6. D
3. A 7. D
4. B

EXPLANATION OF ANSWERS

1. In the opening paragraph of the passage, Sartre is stated to hold that *a man's life acquires meaning only when he makes his choice...and acts accordingly.* Therefore, E is the correct answer. Item A is not mentioned in the passage, nor is Sartre's Existentialism (item B) mentioned in this connection. Items C and D are not referred to

2. In paragraph 3, Sartre states that a writer must act only with the means that are his ...*the written word.* This indicates that D is the correct answer. There is no mention of the ideas contained in items A, B, or C. While he felt that the influence of an institution would not be *fair* to readers, he made no evaluation of *unfavorable*. This discounts item E.

3. The final paragraph states that he ....*was the first recipient of the Nobel Prize for literature to turn it down fully and freely.* Therefore, the correct answer is A. This also serves to eliminate item E from further consideration. Pasternak was put under pressure to reject the prize; and Shaw, after rejecting it, reconsidered; this results in discarding item D. Item B is not considered in the passage. Item C is not so: the Academy was not angered by his refusal.

4. The second paragraph of the passage states that ...*he had been selected by the Swedish Academy of Letters.* Therefore, the correct answer is B. Items A, C, D, and E are incorrect.

5. ...*To add to his pen the influence of an institution is not fair to the reader,* we are told in paragraph 3. Thus, D is the correct answer. This has nothing to do with anonymity, discounting item E. Item C is incorrect since the question itself is based on the fact that he did not accept the prize. There are no grounds for item B, and item A is neither mentioned nor implied.

6. The teachings that form the basis of Sartre's Existentialism were those of Heidegger. Therefore, D is the correct answer. Items A, B, C, and E are incorrect.

7. Items A, B, and E were works of Albert Camus. Item C refers to a film by Jean Genet. D is the correct answer.

TEST 12

PASSAGE

THE RUBAIYAT

Myself when young did eagerly frequent
Doctor and saint, and heard great argument
  About it and about; but evermore
Came out by the same door wherein I went.

QUESTIONS

1. In his youth, the poet

   A. wished to achieve knowledge
   B. wanted to learn about medicine and religion
   C. liked arguments
   D. felt he had nothing to learn from doctor or saint
   E. was not religious

2. The *same door* of the stanza refers to the

   A. door of the temple visited
   B. way of doctor and saint
   C. poet's return to himself
   D. poet emerging with greater knowledge
   E. poet emerging with less knowledge

3. These four lines are an example of what is known as

   A. Rococo
   B. Scansion
   C. the Spenserian stanza
   D. the Rubaiyat stanza
   E. slant rhyme

4. The meter of this stanza is

   A. trochaic
   B. pyrrhic
   C. amphibrachic
   D. iambic
   E. anapestic

5. THE RUBAIYAT was written by

   A. Saki
   B. Omar Khayyam
   C. Rudyard Kipling
   D. Mor Jokai
   E. Boccaccio

6. The famous and excellent poetic translation of this work was done by

   A. Edward Taylor
   B. John Bannister Tabb
   C. Walter Pater
   D. Gerard Hopkins
   E. Edward Fitzgerald

KEY (CORRECT ANSWER)

1. A   4. D
2. C   5. B
3. D   6. E

EXPLANATION OF ANSWERS

1. The poet was, in his youth, in search of knowledge. Therefore, Item A is correct. Items B and C are too narrow in scope. Item D is false because he did *eagerly frequent*. Item E is irrelevant and not mentioned or implied in the stanza.

2. In this phrase, the poet means he left them (doctor and saint) as he found them. He was neither improved nor diminished by their argument. This discounts items B, D, and E. Item C is, therefore, correct. The door mentioned is an intellectual one (item C) rather than a physical one, discounting item A.

3. These lines constitute what is poetically known as the Rubaiyat stanza, so named because the title of this poem is the RUBAIYAT. Therefore, item D is correct. Item A refers to an elaborate 18th century style. Item B is the system of marking lines off into feet. Item C is so named because of Spenser's use of meter. Item E refers to a loose or approximate rhyme.

4. The iamb refers to two syllables: the first unaccented, the second accented. Therefore, item D is correct. Items A, B, C, and E are false. Specifically, item A (trochee) refers to two syllables, the first accented followed by the second unaccented. Item B (pyrrhic) refers to two unaccented syllables. Item C (amphibrach) refers to three syllables, the accented between the two unaccented. Item E (anapest) refers to two unaccented syllables followed by one accented.

5. Item B is correct. The RUBAIYAT was written by Omar Khayyam, a famous Persian poet-astronomer (died 1123?). Items A, C, D, and E are incorrect.

6. Edward Fitzgerald (1809-83) was a British poet and scholar of the Victorian Period in literature. He became famous for what is universally acknowledged as far more than a mere translation of THE RUBAIYAT. Therefore, item E is correct. Items A, B, C, and D are incorrect.

TEST 13

PASSAGE

AND DEATH shall have no dominion.
Dead men naked they shall be one
With the man in the wind and the west moon;
When their bones are picked clean and the clean bones gone,
They shall have stars at elbow and foot;
Though they go mad they shall be sane,
Though they sink through the sea they shall rise again;
Though lovers be lost love shall not;
And death shall have no dominion.

Dylan Thomas

QUESTIONS

1. The poet denies

   A. the existence of death
   B. the authority of death
   C. the inevitability of death
   D. the immortality of man as opposed to the elements of nature
   E. man's immortality

2. Lines _____ and _____ are a part of the same image.

   A. one; two   B. one; three   C. three; five
   D. two; three E. four; six

3. The poet invests the moon and the wind with

   A. omniscience   B. humanity
   C. the bones of dead men D. godliness
   E. the sea and the stars

4. The theme of the poem is that

   A. the living do not forget the dead
   B. the work of the dead becomes a part of eternity
   C. the dead rule over the living in the moon, stars, and seas
   D. love cannot die
   E. death is unimportant

5. Another poem by Dylan Thomas was

   A. THUS THE CITY WAS FOUNDED
   B. DO NOT GO GENTLY INTO THAT GOOD NIGHT
   C. LET US NOW PRAISE FAMOUS MEN
   D. HOW MANY ACTS ARE THERE IN IT
   E. MR. APOLLINAX

6. Thomas died in the decade of the

   A. 1900's   B. 1910's   C. 1920's   D. 1930's   E. 1950's

2 (#13)

KEY (CORRECT ANSWER)

1. B   4. B
2. C   5. B
3. B   6. E

EXPLANATION OF ANSWERS

1. The poet does not deny the existence, actuality, or prospect of death (items A and C) but, rather, its dominion or hegemony. Therefore, item B is correct. Item D is false because the poet unites these two phases or aspects. Item E is affirmed, not denied.

2. The only combination of lines listed above which creates the same image (a celestial one) is that of lines 3 and 5, which constitute item C. Items A, B, D, and E do not produce a similar effect.

3. The poet speaks of ...*the man in the wind and the west moon,* thereby investing them with a kind of humanity. Therefore, item B is correct. Items A and D are not mentioned in the poem. And items C and E are not mentioned in connection with the wind and the moon.

4. Item B is correct. This is distinctly the genius or pith of the poem. There is no mention made of forgetting or ruling, thus discounting items A and C. Item D constitutes merely an element, not the whole of the contribution of those who have gone before us. Were item E correct, it is doubtful that the poem would have been written at all.

5. The poems are ascribed as follows: item A by St. John Perse; item C by James Agee; item D by Gertrude Stein; item E by T.S. Eliot. Item B is the correct answer-it was written by Thomas.

6. Dylan Marlais was born in Wales in 1914 and Thomas died in 1953. Therefore, item E is correct. Items A, B, C, and D are, accordingly, incorrect.

TEST 14

PASSAGE

The wind that rolls a heart on the pavestones of courtyards
An angel that sobs caught in a tree
The column of azure round which twines the marble
Unlock in my darkness emergency exits.

                                            Jean Genet

QUESTIONS

1. Were the first line to read *And the wind that rolls a heart on the pavestones of courtyards,* the poet would

    A. have improved the poem
    B. have created a stronger image
    C. reduced poetry to prose
    D. made the line more mysterious
    E. made the line more abstract

2. The first three lines of the poem

    A. are symbolically in opposition to one another
    B. contain euphemisms
    C. are independent images
    D. are meaningfully united
    E. do not smoothly lead one to the fourth line

3. In the poem, the sky is represented by

    A. the wind   B. an angel
    C. the column   D. emergency exits
    E. marble

4. The poem suggests a condition of

    A. freedom   B. happiness   C. confinement
    D. strife   E. disillusionment

5. While Jean Genet has written many poems, he is better known as a playwright. One of his MOST famous plays is

    A. ENDGAME
    B. THE BALD SOPRANO
    C. CALIGULA
    D. THE BALCONY
    E. WHO'S AFRAID OF VIRGINIA WOOLF?

6. Since the recurrent theme of his works is the condition of man in relation to evil, Genet has often been directly compared with

    A. Cocteau   B. Mallarme
    C. Verlaine   D. St. John Perse
    E. Baudelaire

KEY (CORRECT ANSWER)

1. C
2. D
3. C
4. C
5. D
6. E

EXPLANATION OF ANSWERS

1. Had Genet written this version of the line, he would have been composing prose. The sentence would become a fact, an event precise and dated, rather than a strong, mysterious, poetic image. Therefore, item C is correct. Items A, B, D, and E are false for this reason.

2. The objects of which the first three lines speak resemble each other in the mind of the poet. He wishes to make us aware of this resemblance and, then, leads us to the fourth line, which is explanatory, and informs us why these units are united. Therefore, item D is correct. Item A is false. If they are linked, they cannot be in opposition. Item B is false. If anything, the images are exaggerated rather than understated. Item C is false since the lines are interdependent. Item E is false since the lines do lead the reader straight on to the fourth.

3. In the poem, the sky is represented by *the column of azure*. Therefore, item C is correct. Items A, B, D, and E do not present the reader with the image of the sky and are, accordingly, false.

4. The mention of *emergency exits* being *unlocked* suggest strongly a condition of confinement, of some form of escape being sought. Therefore, item C is correct. Items A and B are in no way indicated, neither in words nor in mood. Item D is not suggested. Item E is untrue because the poem seems to contain an element of hope.

5. Item A is the work of Samuel Beckett; item B is by Eugene Ionesco; item C was written by Albert Camus; item E was authored by Edward Albee. Only item D is the work of Jean Genet and is the correct choice.

6. Item E is correct. Charles Pierre Baudelaire, poet (1821-1867), whose most famous work is FLEURS DU MAL, has shared this comparison with Genet. Items A, B, C, and D are incorrect since none of these men have been involved with this theme.

TEST 15

PASSAGE

It was my thirtieth year to heaven
Woke to my hearing from harbour and neighbor wood
And the mussel pooled and the heron priested shore
    The morning beckon
With water praying and call of seagull and rook And the knock of sailing boats on the net webbed wall
    Myself to set foot
        That second
In the still sleeping town and set forth My birthday began with the water-birds and the birds Of the winged trees flying my name Above the farms and the white horses
    And I rose
    In rainy autumn
And walked abroad in a shower of all my days High tide and the heron dived when I took the road
    Over the border
        And the gates
Of the town closed as the town awoke.

                                                            Dylan Thomas

QUESTIONS

1. The poet was looking at his surroundings

    A. late at night
    B. at a time of day (or night) not stated in the poem
    C. before the people awakened
    D. when everyone was arising
    E. after everyone had gone to sleep

2. The poet speaks mostly of the sights and sounds of the

    A. sea and woods   B. city and the town
    C. border   D. people in the town
    E. sea shore

3. In which, if any, season of the year does the poem take place?

    A. Winter   B. Summer
    C. Autumn   D. Spring
    E. No season is mentioned

4. When the poet says, *And walked abroad in a shower of all my days*, he means he

    A. is walking in the rain
    B. remembers his past
    C. is thinking of his birthday
    D. is walking by the ocean
    E. is thinking of past birthdays

5. The poet, Dylan Thomas, is writing of his native

A. Scotland B. France C. England
D. Ireland E. Wales

6. Another famous poem by Dylan Thomas is 6.____
   A. THE CLOUD IN TROUSERS
   B. EAST CORKER
   C. A SEASON IN HELL
   D. IN MY CRAFT OR SULLEN ART
   E. I, MYSELF

KEY (CORRECT ANSWERS)

1. C 4. B
2. A 5. E
3. C 6. D

EXPLANATION OF ANSWERS

1. The poet uses the words *the still sleeping town* and also the words *And I rose*. These indicate that he awoke before the people of the town, sometime in early morning. Therefore, item C is correct. Items A, B, D, and E are not mentioned or indicated in the poem and are incorrect.

2. The poet speaks of seagulls and sailing boats and of farms and trees. He uses the line *Woke to my hearing from harbour and neighbor wood*. Item A, then, is correct. The town is mentioned only in passing, discounting B and D. Items C and E are both insufficient, and, therefore, unacceptable as correct answers.

3. The poet says, *And I rose in rainy autumn*. Therefore, item C is correct. And the other items, A, B, D, and E, are accordingly false.

4. The *shower of all my days* refers to all his past. Therefore, item B is the correct choice. The poem occurs on the occasion of his birthday (item C) but that is not what the line refers to. Nor is item E correct, because he speaks of ALL his days. Items A and D are obviously not the essence of his thoughts and are incorrect.

5. Thomas lived and wrote in Wales. Item E is correct. Items A, B, C, and D are false.

6. Poems A and E are by Vladimir Mayakovsky. Item B is a poem by T.S. Eliot. Item C is a poem by Rimbaud. Item D is a poem by Dylan Thomas and is the correct answer.

INTERPRETATION OF LITERARY MATERIALS
EXAMINATION SECTION
TEST 1

DIRECTIONS: In the passages that follow, each question or incomplete statement that follows each passage is followed by several suggested answers or completions. Select the one that BEST answers the question or completes the statement. Base your choice in each case on the materials given and on your own understanding of the subject matter.

What things there are to write, if one could only write them! My mind is full of gleaming thoughts; gay moods and mysterious, mothlike meditations hover in my imagination, fanning their painted wings. They would make my fortune if I could catch them; but always the rarest, those freaked with azure and the deepest crimson, flutter away beyond my reach. The ever-baffled chase of these filmy nothings often seems, for one of sober years in a sad world, a trifling occupation. But have I not read of the great Kings of Persia who used to ride out to hawk for butterflies, nor deemed this pastime beneath their royal dignity?

1. The author believes that striving to write well is

    A. inappropriate for a mature person
    B. unappreciated
    C. unnecessary
    D. a trifling occupation
    E. a worthy occupation

2. The author finds that

    A. there [illegible]
    B. he ca[illegible] ...s imagination
    C. he is [illegible]
    D. he [illegible]
    E. it [illegible]

3. The th[illegible]

    A. [illegible]
    B. t[illegible]
    C. th[illegible]
    D. fort[illegible]
    E. the jo[illegible]

KEY (CORRECT ANSWERS)

1. E
2. B
3. C

TEST 2

DIRECTIONS: In the passages that follow, each question or incomplete statement that follows each passage is followed by several suggested answers or completions. Select the one that BEST answers the question or completes the statement. Base your choice in each case on the materials given and on your own understanding of the subject matter.

    The single business of Henry Thoreau, during forty-odd years of eager activity, was to discover an economy calculated to provide a satisfying life. His one concern, that gave to his ramblings in Concord fields a value of high adventure, was to explore the true meaning of wealth. As he understood the problem of economics, there were three possible solutions open to him: to exploit himself, to exploit his fellows, or to reduce the problem to its lowest denominator. The first was quite impossible—to imprison oneself in a treadmill when the morning called to great adventure. To exploit one's fellows seemed to Thoreau's sensitive social conscience an even greater infidelity. Freedom with abstinence seemed to him better than serfdom with material well-being, and he was content to move to Walden Pond and to set about the high business of living, "to front only the essential facts of life and to see what it had to teach." He did not advocate that other men should build cabins and live isolated. He had no wish to dogmatize concerning the best mode of living—each must settle that for himself. But that a satisfying life should be lived, he was vitally concerned. The story of his emancipation from the lower economics is the one romance of his life, and WALDEN is his great book. It is a book in praise of life rather than of Nature, a record of calculating economies that studied saving in order to spend more largely. But it is a book of social criticism as well, in spite of its explicit denial of such a purpose. In considering the true nature of economy, he concluded, with Ruskin, that the cost of a thing is the amount of life which is required in exchange for it, immediately or in the long run. In WALDEN, Thoreau elaborated the text: "The only wealth is life."

1. In Thoreau's opinion, the price of a thing should always be measured in terms of

    A. time   B. effort   C. money
    D. romance   E. life

2. According to Thoreau, the wealth of an individual is measured by

    A. the money he makes
    B. the experience he gains
    C. the amount he saves
    D. the books he writes
    E. his social standing

3. Thoreau's solution to the problem of living was to

    A. study Nature
    B. make other men work for him
    C. work in a mill
    D. live in a simple way
    E. write for a living

4. Thoreau was very

    A. active   B. lazy   C. dissatisfied
    D. unsociable   E. stingy

5. Thoreau's CHIEF aim in life was to 5._____

    A. discover a satisfactory economy
    B. do as little work as possible
    C. convert others to his way of life
    D. write about Nature
    E. live in isolation

6. The theme of this paragraph is 6._____

    A. problems of economics
    B. Thoreau's philosophy of life
    C. WALDEN, Thoreau's greatest work
    D. how Thoreau saved money
    E. life at Walden Pond

KEY (CORRECT ANSWERS)

1.	E	4.	A
2.	B	5.	A
3.	D	6.	B

TEST 3

DIRECTIONS: In the passages that follow, each question or incomplete statement that follows each passage is followed by several suggested answers or completions. Select the one that BEST answers the question or completes the statement. Base your choice in each case on the materials given and on your own understanding of the subject matter.

A moment's reflection will make it clear that one can not live a full, free, influential life in America without argument. No doubt, people often argue on insufficient evidence and for insufficient reasons; no doubt, they often argue on points about which they should rather be thinking and studying; no doubt, they sometimes fancy they are arguing when they are merely wrangling and disputing. But this is only proof that argument is employed badly, that it is misused rather than used skillfully. Argument, at the right moment and for the right purpose and in the right way, is undoubtedly one of the most useful instruments in American life; it is an indispensable means of expressing oneself and impressing others.

1. The theme of this paragraph is

   A. the usefulness of argument
   B. principles of argument
   C. how to win arguments
   D. misuses of argument
   E. need for evidence in argument

2. Argument is an important factor in American life because it gives people a chance to

   A. talk about things of which they know little
   B. influence the ideas of others
   C. develop sufficient evidence
   D. have friendly conversations
   E. use argument at the right time and in the right way

3. Argumentation is being used unwisely when it results in

   A. understanding   B. compromise
   C. deliberation   D. bickering
   E. differences of opinion

KEY (CORRECT ANSWERS)

1. A
2. B
3. D

TEST 4

DIRECTIONS: In the passages that follow, each question or incomplete statement that follows each passage is followed by several suggested answers or completions. Select the one that BEST answers the question or completes the statement. Base your choice in each case on the materials given and on your own understanding of the subject matter.

The characteristic American believes, first, in justice as the foundation of civilized government and society, and, next, in freedom for the individual, so far as that freedom is possible without interference with the equal rights of others. He conceives that both justice and freedom are to be secured through popular respect for the laws enacted by the elected representatives of the people and through the faithful observance of those laws. It should be observed, however, that American justice in general keeps in view the present common good of the vast majority, and the restoration rather than the punishment of the exceptional malignant or defective individual. It is essentially democratic; and especially it finds sufferings inflicted on the innocent unintelligible and abhorrent.

Blind obedience and implicit submission to the will of another do not commend themselves to characteristic Americans. The discipline in which they believe is the voluntary cooperation of many persons in the orderly and effective pursuit of common ends. Thus, they submit willingly to any restrictions on individual liberty which can be shown to be necessary to the preservation of the public health, and they are capable of the most effective cooperation at need in business, sports, and war.

1. The American people believe in

    A. unquestioning obedience to their laws
    B. strict discipline
    C. liberty without restraint
    D. subservience to the President
    E. working together for a necessary purpose

2. American justice emphasizes

    A. the welfare of the minority
    B. retaliation for disobedience
    C. rehabilitation of wrongdoers
    D. the sufferings of the innocent
    E. punishment of criminals

3. The PRIMARY element in the American way of life is

    A. the right to vote
    B. freedom
    C. willingness to follow leaders
    D. justice
    E. popular respect for laws

4. The theme of this selection is
    A. American justice
    B. a plea for cooperation
    C. the basis of American democracy
    D. the American government
    E. liberty as the foundation of government

KEY (CORRECT ANSWERS)

1. E
2. C
3. D
4. C

TEST 5

DIRECTIONS: In the passages that follow, each question or incomplete statement that follows each passage is followed by several suggested answers or completions. Select the one that BEST answers the question or completes the statement. Base your choice in each case on the materials given and on your own understanding of the subject matter.

The change in the treatment of his characters is a significant index to Shakespeare's growth as a dramatist. In the earlier plays, his men and women are more engaged with external forces than with internal struggles. In as excellent an early tragedy as ROMEO AND JULIET, the hero fights more with outside obstacles than with himself. In the great later tragedies, the internal conflict is more emphasized, as in the cases of HAMLET and MACBETH. He grew to care less for mere incident, for plots based on mistaken identity, as in the COMEDY OF ERRORS; he became more and more interested in the delineation of character, in showing the effect of evil on Macbeth and his wife, of jealousy on OTHELLO, of indecision on Hamlet, as well as in exploring the ineffectual attempts of many of his characters to escape the consequences of their acts.

1. The development of Shakespeare as a dramatist is MOST clearly revealed in his

    A. improved treatment of complications
    B. increased use of involved plots
    C. handling of emotional conflicts
    D. increased variety of plot
    E. decreased dependency on historical characters

2. In his later plays, Shakespeare became interested in

    A. plots based on mistaken identity
    B. great characters from history
    C. the history of his country
    D. the study of human nature
    E. the struggle of the hero with external forces

3. The theme of this paragraph is

    A. comedies and tragedies of Shakespeare
    B. Shakespeare's best plays
    C. Shakespeare's development as a dramatist
    D. the moral aspects of Shakespeare's later plays
    E. Shakespeare's interest in good and evil

KEY (CORRECT ANSWERS)

1. C
2. D
3. C

TEST 6

DIRECTIONS: In the passages that follow, each question or incomplete statement that follows each passage is followed by several suggested answers or completions. Select the one that BEST answers the question or completes the statement. Base your choice in each case on the materials given and on your own understanding of the subject matter.

Solitude is a great chastener when once you accept it. It quietly eliminates all sorts of traits that were a part of you - among others, the desire to pose, to keep your best foot forever in evidence, to impress people as being something you would like to have them think you are even when you aren't. Some men I know are able to pose even in solitude; had they valets they no doubt would be heroes to them. But I find it the hardest kind of work myself; and as I am lazy, I have stopped trying. To act without an audience is so tiresome and profitless that you gradually give it up and at last forget how to act at all. For you become more interested in making the acquaintance of yourself as you really are, which is a meeting that, in the haunts of men, rarely takes place. It is gratifying, for example, to discover that you prefer to be clean rather than dirty even when there is no one but God to care which you are; just as it is amusing to note, however, that for scrupulous cleanliness, you are not inclined to make superhuman sacrifices, although you used to believe you were. Clothes, you learn, with something of a shock, have for you no interest whatsoever....You learn to regard dress merely as covering, a precaution. For its color and its cut you care nothing.

1. The activities of everyday life seldom give us the chance to

    A. learn our own peculiarities
    B. keep our best foot forward
    C. impress people
    D. dress as we would like
    E. be immaculately clean

2. The desire to appear well-dressed USUALLY depends upon

    A. an audience
    B. industriousness
    C. personal pride
    D. the need for cleanliness
    E. a fondness for acting

3. In solitude, clothes

    A. constitute one item that pleases the valet
    B. make one careless
    C. are part of acting
    D. are valued for their utility only
    E. are tiresome

4. A desire to appear at your best is a trait that

    A. goes with laziness
    B. may disappear when you are alone
    C. depends primarily on clothes
    D. is inhuman
    E. is evil

5. The theme of this paragraph is 5.____
   A. carelessness in clothes
   B. acting without an audience
   C. discoveries through solitude
   D. showing off to best advantage
   E. being a hero to yourself

KEY (CORRECT ANSWERS)

1. A
2. A
3. D
4. B
5. C

TEST 7

DIRECTIONS: In the passages that follow, each question or incomplete statement that follows each passage is followed by several suggested answers or completions. Select the one that BEST answers the question or completes the statement. Base your choice in each case on the materials given and on your own understanding of the subject matter.

In width of scope, Yeats far exceeds any of his contemporaries. He is the only poet since the 18th century who has been a public man in his own country and the only poet since Milton who has been a public man at a time when his country was involved in a struggle for political liberty. This may not seem an important matter, but it is a question whether the kind of life lived by poets for the last two hundred years or so has not been one great reason for the drift of poetry away from the life of the community as a whole, and the loss of touch with tradition. Once the life of contemplation has been divorced from the life of action, or from real knowledge of men of action, something is lost which it is difficult to define, but which leaves poetry enfeebled and incomplete. Yeats responded with all his heart as a young man to the reality and the romance of Ireland's struggle, but he lived to be completely disillusioned about the value of the Irish rebellion. He saw his dreams of liberty blotted out in horror by "the innumerable clanging wings that have put out the moon." It brought him to the final conclusion of the futility of all discipline that is not of the whole being, and of "how base at moments of excitement are minds without culture"; but he remained a man to whom the life of action always meant something very real.

1. According to the writer of the paragraph, great poetry is MOST often produced by poets who

    A. are involved in the problems of life around them
    B. spend their time in contemplation
    C. drift away from the community
    D. break away from tradition
    E. take part in war

2. The writer implies that, as compared with older poetry, present-day poetry is more

    A. complete B. romantic C. alive
    D. ineffectual E. comprehensive

3. Yeats was PRIMARILY a

    A. soldier B. man of action
    C. dreamer D. rigid disciplinarian
    E. politician

4. The theme of this paragraph is

    A. basis of true poetry
    B. the necessity of culture
    C. action versus contemplation
    D. Yeats as a poet and patriot
    E. Yeats' part in the Irish rebellion

KEY (CORRECT ANSWERS)

1. A
2. D
3. B
4. D

TEST 8

DIRECTIONS: In the passages that follow, each question or incomplete statement that follows each passage is followed by several suggested answers or completions. Select the one that BEST answers the question or completes the statement. Base your choice in each case on the materials given and on your own understanding of the subject matter.

Only twice in literary history has there been a great period of tragedy, in the Athens of Pericles and in Elizabethan England. What these two periods had in common, two thousand years and more apart in time, that they expressed themselves in the same fashion, may give us some hint of the nature of tragedy, for far from being periods of darkness and defeat, each was a time when life was seen exalted, a time of thrilling and unfathomable possibilities. They held their heads high, those men who conquered at Marathon and Salamis and those who fought Spain and saw the Great Armada sink. The world was a place of wonder; manking was beauteous; life was lived on the crest of the wave. More than all, the poignant joy of heroism had stirred men's hearts. Not stuff for tragedy, would you say? But on the crest of the wave, one must feel either tragically or joyously; one cannot feel tamely. The temper of mind that sees tragedy in life has not for its opposite the temper that sees joy. The opposite pole to the tragic view of life is the sordid view. When humanity is seen as devoid of dignity and significance, trivial, mean, and sunk in dreary hopelessness, then the spirit of tragedy departs.

1. In an age of glory, one

   A. is not indifferent
   B. usually feels tragic
   C. feels happy
   D. is apathetic
   E. feels mean and hopeless

2. The two periods in which great tragedies were written were periods of

   A. gloom B. serenity C. defeat
   D. confusion E. valor

3. The mental attitude that finds tragedy in life is characterized by

   A. sordidness B. indifference C. exaltation
   D. triviality E. hopelessness

4. The theme of this paragraph is

   A. two thousand years of tragedy
   B. Periclean Athens
   C. the tragedy of war
   D. the psychology of happiness
   E. mainsprings of tragic drama

KEY (CORRECT ANSWERS)

1. A
2. E
3. C
4. E

TEST 9

DIRECTIONS: In the passages that follow, each question or incomplete statement that follows each passage is followed by several suggested answers or completions. Select the one that BEST answers the question or completes the statement. Base your choice in each case on the materials given and on your own understanding of the subject matter.

There are few books which go with midnight, solitude, and a candle. It is much easier to say what does not please us then than what is exactly right. The book must be, anyhow, something benedictory by a sinning fellow man. Cleverness would be repellent at such an hour. Cleverness, anyhow, is the level of mediocrity today, we are all too infernally clever. The first witty and perverse paradox blows out the candle. Only the sick mind craves cleverness, as a morbid body turns to drink. The late candle throws its beams a great distance, and its rays make transparent much that seemed massy and important. The mind at rest beside that light, when the house is asleep, and the consequential affairs of the urgent world have diminished to their right proportions because we seem them distantly from another and a more tranquil place in the heavens, where duty, honor, witty arguments, controversial logic on great questions, appear such as will leave hardly a trace of fossil in the indurated mud which will cover them—the mind then smiles at cleverness. For though at that hour the body may be dog-tired, the mind is white and lucid, like that of a man from whom a fever has abated. It is bare of illusions. It has a sharp focus, small and starlike, as a clear and lonely flame left burning by the altar of a shrine from which all have gone but one. A book which approaches that light in the privacy of that place must come, as it were, with open and honest pages.

1. At midnight in the solitude of one's room, the mind is

    A. tired B. keen C. sick
    D. troubled E. clever

2. The author considers the average book of today

    A. inane B. sinful C. benedictory
    D. restful E. open and honest

3. Naming the qualities of a book suitable for reading when one retires is

    A. logical B. a clever job
    C. difficult D. like lighting a candle
    E. tiresome

4. To make good reading at bedtime, a book must be

    A. light B. witty C. controversial
    D. historical E. straightforward

5. The theme of this paragraph is

    A. reading by candlelight
    B. books for convalescents
    C. not a time to read
    D. books for tired minds
    E. books for midnight reading

KEY (CORRECT ANSWERS)

1. B
2. A
3. C
4. E
5. E

TEST 10

DIRECTIONS: In the passages that follow, each question or incomplete statement that follows each passage is followed by several suggested answers or completions. Select the one that BEST answers the question or completes the statement. Base your choice in each case on the materials given and on your own understanding of the subject matter.

Few things are move stimulating than the sight of the forceful wings of large birds cleaving the vagueness of air and making the piled clouds a mere background for their concentrated life. The peregrine falcon, becalmed in the blue depths, cruises across space without a tremor of his wide wings. Wild geese beat up in the sky in a compact wedge. Primeval force is in their strongly moving wings and their beautiful, outstretched necks, in their power of untiring effort, and the eager search of their wild hearts for the free spaces they love. The good fellowship of swift, united action, the joy of ten thousand that move as one, is in the flight of flocks of birds. When seagulls flash up from the water with every wing at full stretch, there is no deliberation; it is as if each bird saw a sweeping arc before it and followed its individual way faithfully. The unerring judgment of the grand curve when the wings are so near and yet never collide, the speed of the descent, are pure poetry.

1. He admires the ability of seagulls to

   A. coordinate their flight
   B. reach great heights
   C. stretch their wings
   D. rise from the water
   E. dive swiftly

2. The flight of the wild goose, as compared with that of the falcon, is MORE

   A. active
   B. beautiful
   C. poetic
   D. deliberate
   E. graceful

3. The author finds the sight of flying birds

   A. inspiring
   B. awesome
   C. joyful
   D. consoling
   E. primitive

4. The author admires the falcon's

   A. wild freedom
   B. effortless flight
   C. united action
   D. primitive force
   E. unerring judgment

5. The theme of this paragraph is

   A. our wild birds
   B. the superb falcon
   C. the beauty of flight
   D. citizens of the sky
   E. the lure of the wild

KEY (CORRECT ANSWERS)

1. A
2. A
3. A
4. B
5. C

TEST 11

DIRECTIONS: In the passages that follow, each question or incomplete statement that follows each passage is followed by several suggested answers or completions. Select the one that BEST answers the question or completes the statement. Base your choice in each case on the materials given and on your own understanding of the subject matter.

As we know the short story today, it is largely a product of the nineteenth and twentieth centuries and its development parallels the rapid development of industrialism in America. We have been a busy people, busy principally in evolving a production system supremely efficient. Railroads and factories have blossomed almost overnight; mines and oil fields have been discovered and exploited; mechanical inventions by the thousand have been made and perfected. Speed has been an essential element in our endeavors, and it has affected our lives, our very natures. Leisurely reading has been, for most Americans, impossible. As with our meals, we have grabbed bits of reading standing up, cafeteria style, and gulped down cups of sentiment on the run. We have had to read while hanging on to a strap in a swaying trolley car or in a rushing subway or while tending to a clamoring telephone switchboard. Our popular magazine has been our literary automat, and its stories have often been no more substantial than sandwiches.

1. From this selection, one would assume that the author's attitude toward short stories is one of

   A. approval
   B. indifference
   C. contempt
   D. impartiality
   E. regret

2. The short story has developed because of Americans'

   A. reactions against the classics
   B. need for reassurance
   C. lack of culture
   D. lack of education
   E. taste for speed

3. The short story today owes its popularity to its

   A. settings
   B. plots
   C. style
   D. length
   E. characters

4. The theme of this paragraph is

   A. *quick-lunch* literature
   B. life in the machine age
   C. culture in modern life
   D. reading while traveling
   E. the development of industrialism

KEY (CORRECT ANSWERS)

1. E
2. E
3. D
4. A

TEST 12

DIRECTIONS: In the passages that follow, each question or incomplete statement that follows each passage is followed by several suggested answers or completions. Select the one that BEST answers the question or completes the statement. Base your choice in each case on the materials given and on your own understanding of the subject matter.

    If Shakespeare needs any excuse for the exuberance of his language (the high key in which he pitched most of his dramatic dialogue), it should be remembered that he was doing on the plastic stage of his own day what on the pictorial stage of our day is not so much required. Shakespeare's dramatic figures stood out on a platform-stage, without background, with the audience on three sides of it. And the whole of his atmosphere and environment had to come from the gestures and language of the actors. When they spoke, they provided their own scenery, which we now provide for them. They had to do a good deal more (when they spoke) than actors have to do today in order to give the setting. They carried the scenery on their backs, as it were, and spoke it in words.

1. The nature of the stage for which Shakespeare wrote made it necessary for him to

   A. employ only highly dramatic situations
   B. depend on scenery owned by the actors themselves
   C. have the actors shift the scenery
   D. create atmosphere through the dialogue
   E. restrict backgrounds to familiar types of scenes

2. In comparison with actors of Shakespeare's time, actors of today

   A. carry the settings in their words
   B. pitch their voices in a lower key
   C. depend more on elaborate settings
   D. have to do more to make the setting clear
   E. use many gestures

3. The theme of this paragraph is

   A. the scenery of the Elizabethan stage
   B. the importance of actors in the Shakespearean drama
   C. the influence of the Elizabethan stage on Shakespeare's style
   D. the importance of words
   E. suitable gestures for the Elizabethan stage

KEY (CORRECT ANSWERS)

1. D
2. C
3. C

TEST 13

DIRECTIONS: In the passages that follow, each question or incomplete statement that follows each passage is followed by several suggested answers or completions. Select the one that BEST answers the question or completes the statement. Base your choice in each case on the materials given and on your own understanding of the subject matter.

It is no secret that I am not one of those naturalists who suffer from cities, or affect to do so, nor do I find a city unnatural or uninteresting, or a rubbish heap of follies. It has always seemed to me that there is something more than mechanically admirable about a train that arrives on time, a fire department that comes when you call it, a light that leaps into the room at a touch, and a clinic that will fight for the health of a penniless man and mass for him the agencies of mercy, the x-ray, the precious radium, the anesthetics and the surgical skill. For, beyond any pay these services receive, stands out the pride in perfect performance. And above all, I admire the noble impersonality of civilization that does not inquire where the recipient stands on religion or politics or race. I call this beauty, and I call it spirit—not some mystical soulfulness that nobody can define, but the spirit of man, that has been a million years a-growing.

1. The author implies that efficient operation of public utilities is

    A. expensive
    B. of no special interest
    C. admired by most naturalists
    D. mechanically commendable
    E. spiritual in quality

2. The aspect of city life MOST commendable to this author is its

    A. punctuality   B. free benefits
    C. impartial service   D. mechanical improvement
    E. health clinics

3. The author makes a defense of

    A. cities   B. prompt trains
    C. rural life   D. nature
    E. free clinics

4. The services rendered by city agencies are given

    A. only for pay
    B. on time
    C. only to people having a certain political allegiance
    D. to everybody
    E. to the spirit of man

5. The theme of this paragraph is

    A. the spirit of the city
    B. advantages of a city home
    C. disagreement among naturalists
    D. admirable characteristics of cities
    E. tolerance in the city

KEY (CORRECT ANSWERS)

1. E
2. C
3. A
4. D
5. D

TEST 14

DIRECTIONS: In the passages that follow, each question or incomplete statement that follows each passage is followed by several suggested answers or completions. Select the one that BEST answers the question or completes the statement. Base your choice in each case on the materials given and on your own understanding of the subject matter.

The annual survey of chemistry published by the American Chemical Society attributes the vast change in warfare to the airplane and, above all, to the motor fuels of today. We never think of gasoline as an explosive, yet it has to some extent taken the place of the artillery propellants of a quarter of a century ago. A bomber is hardly a gun, but it certainly performs the function of one, with a range of many hundred miles.

About fifteen years ago, we began to hear of iso-octane, a fuel used to measure antiknock qualities of high-compression gasoline. It was ideal for airplanes but quantity production was not practical Now we make lakes of it. Its performance is so remarkable that the planes propelled by it can carry loads that would have been inconceivable only ten years ago. As a result, octane numbers and indexes of antiknock properties have lost much of their former significance. It will probably be necessary to adopt some new standard. If we relate size and weight of engine to octane number, a truer picture of what aviation fuels really are is obtained. For each pound of weight, aviation engines of today produce, respectively, 100 percent and 50 percent more power than could those of 1918 and 1930.

1. The writer suggests that gasoline may be considered an explosive because

    A. it produces high compression
    B. modern bombing planes are essentially long-range guns
    C. guns now have greater range
    D. iso-octane is now manufactured in quantity
    E. it has replaced explosives in cannons

2. The proposed standard for measuring the quality of motor fuels is the

    A. ratio of power to weight
    B. antiknock index
    C. iso-octane number
    D. load-carrying ability
    E. relation of engine weight and size to octane number

3. Per pound of weight, the average engine now produces

    A. very much iso-octane
    B. high compression
    C. twice as much power as in 1930
    D. double the power of 1918
    E. 100 percent efficiency

4. The theme of this selection is
    A. the chemist speeds the airplane
    B. mass production of iso-octane
    C. improving the gasoline engine
    D. changing methods in warfare
    E. gasoline as an explosive

KEY (CORRECT ANSWERS)

1. B
2. E
3. D
4. A

TEST 15

DIRECTIONS: In the passages that follow, each question or incomplete statement that follows each passage is followed by several suggested answers or completions.
Select the one that BEST answers the question or completes the statement.
Base your choice in each case on the materials given and on your own understanding of the subject matter.

Once the rivers of America slid undisturbed between their banks, save when a birch canoe, manned by stolid Indians, sewed a narrow seam in the water. Then came a day when our rivers were broad highways filled with packets, lumber rafts, and houseboats. There were years when the rivers languished, deserted by the great commerce they had carried; years, too, of floods and devastation. Today, there is a difference. Efforts are being made to tame the untamed, to yoke the slow-sliding rivers to useful purpose. Dams are being built that will end the tragic flooding of the lowlands. Wasteful torrents are being taught economy, taught to irrigate the lands that lie fallow, needing only water to bring them to fruitfulness. The life-giving fluid to renewed utility is being fed into these rivers of ours, and they are again becoming a vital and integral part of our economy.

1. A MAJOR reason for flood control is

    A. provision of suitable streams for the Indians
    B. profits for the public utilities
    C. conservation of farming areas
    D. relief of unemployment
    E. restoring river commerce

2. America's rivers have

    A. been a steady commercial asset
    B. helped protect us against invasion
    C. brought serious destruction through floods
    D. alternated frequently between periods of usefulness and of destruction or neglect
    E. suffered complete neglect as railroads developed

3. Failing to utilize a country's rivers

    A. is economically wasteful
    B. makes the rivers sluggish
    C. restores their scenic beauty
    D. renews their picturesque traffic
    E. causes wasteful torrents

4. For the safety of property and people, rivers must be

    A. made into highways
    B. used for irrigation
    C. allowed to lie fallow
    D. utilized for commerce
    E. brought under control

5. The theme of this paragraph is
    A. from Indian canoe to modern boat
    B. conservation and our rivers
    C. the utility of water
    D. changing river traffic
    E. rivers, dams, and the public utilities

5.__

KEY (CORRECT ANSWERS)

1. C
2. C
3. A
4. E
5. B

ANALYSIS AND INTERPRETATION OF LITERATURE
EXAMINATION SECTION
TEST 1

DIRECTIONS: Read the following poems. The questions which follow are based on these poems. *PRINT THE LETTER OF THE CORRECT ANSWER IN THE SPACE AT THE RIGHT.*

Questions 1-3.

POEM

When I consider Life and its few years—
A wisp of fog betwixt us and the sun;
A call to battle, and the battle done
Ere the last echo dies within our ears;
A rose choked in the grass; an hour of fears;
The gusts that past a darkening shore do beat;
The burst of music down an unlistening street,—
I wonder at the idleness of tears.
Ye old, old dead, and ye of yesternight,
Chieftains, and bards, and keepers of the sheep,
By every cup of sorrow that you had,
Loose me from tears, and make me see aright
How each hath back what once he stayed to weep:
Homer his sight, David his little lad!

QUESTIONS

1. The statement which *most closely* summarizes the intellectual content of the poem is:

   A. It is idle to weep because life is so short and because we will one day get back what we have lost.
   B. Weeping is an idle pastime. Forego it and heed the call to battle before the battle is done.
   C. Tears blind us to the loveliness and music of life. Stop weeping and, like David and Homer, see again Nature's grandeur.
   D. The poet thinks of life as mists, battle cries, music, roses, rulers, poets, keepers of the sheep, and, like David, recognizes the futility of tears.

2. The *most appropriate* title for the poem is:

   A. *A Wisp of Fog*   B. *Tears*
   C. *Battle Cry*   D. *What Homer Stayed to Weep*

3. The poem is written in

   A. dactyllic pentameter   B. anapestic tetrameter
   C. iambic pentameter   D. trochaic tetrameter

Questions 4-5.

POEM

The wisdom of the world is this: to say "There is
No other wisdom but to gulp what time can give"...
To guard no inward vision winged with mysteries;
To hear no voices haunt the hurrying hours we live;
To keep no faith with ghostly friends; never to know
Vigils of sorrow crowned when loveless passions fade...
From wisdom such as this to find my gloom I go,
Companioned by those powers who keep me unafraid.

QUESTIONS

4. The theme of the poem may BEST be expressed as:

    A. Gather ye rosebuds while ye may
    B. Holding fast to one's ideals gives meaning to life even at the brink of death
    C. There is no faith worth clinging to
    D. A faith unfaithful keeps us falsely true

5. The *most appropriate* title for this poem is:

    A. *To the Worldly-Wise*   B. *The Wisdom of the World*
    C. *I Am the Captain of My Fate*   D. *Vigils of Sorrow*

Questions 6-8.

POEM

Socrates' ghost must haunt me now,
Notorious death has let him go,
He comes to me with a clumsy bow,
Saying in his disused voice,
That I do not know I do not know,
The mechanical whims of appetite
Are all that I have of conscious choice,
The butterfly caged in electric light
Is my only day in the world's great night,
Love is not love, it is a child
Sucking his thumb and biting his lip,
But grasp it all, there may be more!
From the topless sky to the bottomless floor
With the heavy head and the fingertip:
All is not blind, obscene, and poor.
Socrates stands by me stockstill,
Teaching hope to my flickering will,
Pointing to the sky's inexorable blue
—Old Noumenon, come true, come true!

QUESTIONS

6. Each of the following expressions used in the above poem is acceptably explained EXCEPT:

    A. "That I do not know I do not know."—The wise man knows he knows nothing
    B. "The butterfly caged in electric light
       Is my only day in the world's great night," The mind really understands only physical phenomena
    C. conscious choice—free will
    D. inexorable—unwavering

7. The theme of this poem is *BEST* expressed by:

    A. We are creatures of physical impulses only
    B. "All's right with the world"
    C. Man's striving to understand the universe is a powerful incentive through the ages
    D. Socrates' inquiring spirit points the way to heaven

8. The poem

    A. is a sonnet
    B. is written in blank verse
    C. is written in free verse
    D. has a varying metrical pattern

Questions 9-11.

POEM
DISCOVERY

We told of him as one who should have soared
And seen for us the devastating light
Whereof there is not either day or night,
And shared with us the glamour of the
Word That fell once upon Amos to record
For men at ease in Zion, when the sight
Of ills obscured aggrieved him and the might
Of Hamath was a warning of the Lord.

Assured somehow that he would make us wise,
Our pleasure was to wait; and our surprise
Was hard when we confessed the dry return
Of his regret. For we were still to learn
That earth has not a school where we may go
For wisdom, or for more than we may know.

QUESTIONS

9. The "discovery" is:

   A. A prophet is without honor in his own country
   B. A poor teacher fails to inspire
   C. A wise man regrets he cannot impart wisdom to others
   D. Amos rebuked those at ease in Zion

10. Each of the following expressions as used in the poem is acceptably explained EXCEPT:

    A. Word—the message of God
    B. Amos—a famous psalmist
    C. Hamath—an enemy of ancient Israel
    D. confessed—acknowledged

11. This poem is composed of

    A. heroic couplets
    B. blank verse
    C. free verse
    D. lines in iambic pentameter with a definite rhyme scheme

Questions 12-15.

POEM

Move him in the sun—
Gently its touch awoke him once,
At home, whispering of fields unsown,
Always it woke him, even in France,
Until this morning and this snow.
If anything might rouse him now
The kind old sun will know.
Think how it wakes the seeds,—
Woke, once, the clays of a cold star.
Are limbs, so dear-achieved, are sides,
Full-nerved—still warm—too hard to stir?
Was it for this the clay grew tall?
—O what made fatuous sunbeams toil
To break earth's sleep at all?

QUESTIONS

12. Of the following, the one that *CANNOT* be surmised from the context is that the man had

    A. died suddenly
    B. died away from home
    C. died in battle
    D. at one time toiled with his hands

13. Of the following, the title that *BEST* expresses the thought and mood of the poem is:

    A. *Futility*
    B. *The Giver of Life and Death*
    C. *Resignation*
    D. *Sun, Man and Earth*

14. The poem does NOT deal with the

    A. possibility of reviving the dead
    B. meaning of life
    C. purpose of evolution
    D. inhumanity of man

15. Of the following, the expression *most nearly* synonymous with *fatuous,* as used in the poem, is

    A. urbane
    B. ineffectual
    C. benign
    D. untiring

Questions 16-19.

POEM

Only the diamond and the diamond's dust
Can render up the diamond unto Man;
One and invulnerable as it began
Had it endured, but for the treacherous thrust
That laid its hard heart open, as it must,
And ground it down and fitted it to span
A turbaned brow or fret an ivory fan,
Lopped of its stature, pared of its proper crust.
So Man, by all the wheels of heaven unscored,
Man, the stout ego, the exuberant mind
No edge could cleave, no acid could consume,
Being split along the vein by its own kind,
Gives over, rolls upon the palm abhorred,
Is set in brass on the swart thumb of Doom.

QUESTIONS

16. Of the following, the one that BEST expresses the thought of the poem is:

    A. Man's defiance of natural forces
    B. Man's improvement of the raw treasures of the earth
    C. Man's admirable ability flawed by his own weakness
    D. The eventual conquest of Man and Nature by a superior force

17. The "diamond's dust," referred to in line 1 is, most probably,

    A. an abrasive used to polish diamonds
    B. a substance located on the surface of the earth in areas where diamonds are found
    C. the "proper crust" of line 8
    D. Man's restless and ambitious nature

18. In the poem, comparisons are drawn between all of the following EXCEPT

    A. the diamond and Man
    B. "the diamond's dust" and "his own kind"
    C. "a turbaned brow" and "the swart thumb"
    D. "the wheels of heaven" and "one and invulnerable"

19. Of the following words, as used in the poem, the one which is INCORRECTLY defined is:

    A. invulnerable—unassailable   B. fret—adorn
    C. unscored—unmarked   D. swart—calloused

Questions 20-22.

PASSAGE

One fact is plain: we have not yet experienced the establishment of a universal state, in spite of two desperate efforts by the Germans to impose one upon us in the first half of the present century—and an equally desperate attempt by Napoleonic France a hundred years earlier. Another fact is equally plain: there is among us a profound and heartfelt aspiration for the establishment, not of a universal state, but of some form of world order, akin perhaps to the Homonoia or Concord preached in vain by certain Hellenic statesmen and philosophers during the Hellenic time of troubles, which will secure the blessings of a universal state without its deadly curse. The curse of a universal state is that it is the result of a successful knockout blow delivered by one sole surviving member of a group of contending military Powers. It is a product of that "salvation by the sword" which we have seen to be no salvation at all. What we are looking for is a free consent of free peoples to dwell together in unity, and to make, uncoerced, the far-reaching adjustments and concessions without which this ideal cannot be realized in practice. There is no need to enlarge upon this theme, which is the commonplace of thousands of contemporary disquisitions. The astonishing prestige enjoyed by the American President Wilson in Europe—though not in his own country-during the few short months preceding and following the armistice of November 1918 was a measure of the aspirations of our world. President Wilson was addressed for the most part in prose; the best-known surviving testimonials to Augustus are in the verses of Virgil and Horace. But, prose or verse, the spirit animating these two outpourings of faith, hope and thanksgiving was manifestly the same. The outcome, however, was different. Augustus succeeded in providing his world with a universal state; Wilson failed to provide his with something better.

That low man goes on adding one to one;
   His hundred's soon hit.
This high man, aiming at a million,
   Misses a unit.

QUESTIONS

20. *The BEST title for the above passage is:*

   A. *Swords into Ploughshares*
   B. *Federation of the World*
   C. *Hitch Your Wagon to a Star*
   D. *Universal State versus World Order*

21. Each of the following references is correctly explained EXCEPT:

   A. "Hellenic time of troubles"-wars between Greek states for hegemony
   B. Virgil-Greek epic poet
   C. Horace-Roman odist
   D. Augustus-emperor during the golden age of literature

22. Of the following, the LEAST defensible inference to be drawn from the passage is:

   A. The Soviet dream of world conquest was doomed to failure.
   B. The survivor in a universal state must have subjected all rivals
   C. The United Nations may be working successfully toward establishing world order
   D. Europe in 1918 was ahead of America in acknowledging international statesmanship

Questions 23-28.

PASSAGE I

"After all, sir, we must submit to this idea, that the true principle of a republic is, that the people should choose whom they please to govern them. Representation is imperfect in proportion as the current of popular favor is checked. This great source of free government, popular election, should be perfectly pure, and the most unbounded liberty allowed. Where this principle is adhered to; where, in the organization of the government, the legislative, executive, and judicial branches are rendered distinct; where, again, the legislature is divided into separate houses, and the operations of each are controlled by various checks and balances, and above all, by the vigilance and weight of the state governments,—to talk of tyranny, and the subversion of our liberties, is to speak the language of enthusiasm. This balance between the national and state governments ought to be dwelt on with peculiar attention, as it is of the utmost importance. It forms a double security to the people. If one encroaches on their rights, they will find a powerful protection in the other. Indeed, they will both be prevented from overpassing their constitutional limits, by a certain rivalship which will ever subsist between them. I am persuaded that a firm union is as necessary to perpetuate our liberties as it is to make us respectable; and experience will probably prove that the national government will be as natural a guardian of our freedom as the state legislature(s) themselves."

Alexander Hamilton

PASSAGE II

"An honorable gentleman from New York has remarked that the idea of danger to state governments can originate in a distempered fancy; he stated that they were necessary component parts of the system, and informed us how the President and senators were to be elected; his conclusion is, that the liberties of the people can not be endangered. I shall only observe, that, however fanciful these apprehensions may appear to him, they have made serious impressions upon some of the greatest and best men. Our fears arise from the experience of all ages and our knowledge of the dispositions of mankind. I believe the gentleman can not point out an instance of the rights of the people remaining for a long period inviolate.... Sir, wherever the revenues and the military force are, there will rest the power: the members or the head will prevail, as one or the other possesses these advantages... Sir, if you do not give the state governments a power to protect themselves, if you leave them no other check upon Congress than the power of appointing senators, they will certainly be overcome, like the barons of whom the gentleman has spoken. Neither our civil nor militia officers will afford many advantages of opposition against the national government: if they have any powers, it will ever be difficult to concentrate them, or give them a uniform direction. Their influence will hardly be felt, while the greater number of lucrative and honorable places, in the gift of the United States, will establish an influence which will prevail in every part of the continent."

John Lansing

QUESTIONS

23. Which one of the groups (A-E) listed below indicates statements that are consistent with Mr. Hamilton's arguments for establishing a centralized government?
    I. A centralized government would increase the nation's prestige.
    II. A centralized government would provide a double security for individual liberty.
    III. The rivalry between Federal and state governments would lead to friction between the states.
    IV. The state governments would have even more influence in checking the power of the national government than would the system of checks and balances.
    V. The maintenance of a standing army would promote centralized power.
    The CORRECT answer is:

    A. I, II, III, IV   B. I, II, IV   C. I, II, V   D. II, III, IV   E. III, IV, V

24. Which one of the groups (A-E) listed below indicates Mr. Lansing's reasons for believing the Federal government would overshadow the state governments?
    I. Control of patronage
    II. Feeling of nationalism
    III. Power of the civil officers
    IV. Power to raise an army
    V. Power to tax
    The CORRECT answer is:

    A. I, II, III   B. I, II, IV   C. I, IV, V   D. II, III, IV   E. II, III, V

25. Which one of the groups (A-E) listed below indicate topics on which Mr. Hamilton and Mr. Lansing disagree?
    I. Ability of the states to check national power
    II. Dangers to individual rights in a Federal system
    III. Faith in the state rather than in the national government
    IV. Method of appointing senators
    V. Necessity for a Federal union
    The CORRECT answer is:

    A. I, II, III   B. I, III, V   C. II, III, IV   D. II, IV, V   E. III, IV, V

26. According to the passage, which one of the following did Mr. Hamilton believe?

    A. States should determine voting qualifications.
    B. Suffrage should be granted to all adult males.
    C. Suffrage should be limited.
    D. Suffrage should be unrestricted.
    E. United States Senators should be appointed by the state legislatures.

27. On which one of the following topics did John Lansing base his arguments for state sovereignty?

    A. Antipathy toward Hamilton
    B. Danger of excessive Federal taxation
    C. Distrust of contemporary leaders
    D. Examples from past history
    E. Personal experience under the Articles of Confederation

28. Which one of the following men would have been MOST NEARLY in agreement with the views expressed by Mr.Lansing in the above passage?

    A. Abraham Lincoln
    B. Andrew Jackson
    C. George Washington
    D. John Calhoun
    E. Thomas Paine

KEY (CORRECT ANSWERS)

1. A	11. D	21. B
2. B	12. C	22. A
3. C	13. A	23. B
4. B	14. D	24. C
5. B	15. B	25. A
6. A	16. C	26. D
7. C	17. A	27. D
8. D	18. D	28. D
9. C	19. D	
10. B	20. D	

ANALYSIS AND INTERPRETATION OF LITERATURE
EXAMINATION SECTION
TEST 1

DIRECTIONS: Each question or incomplete statement is followed by several suggested answers or completions. Select the one that BEST answers the question or completes the statement. *PRINT THE LETTER OF THE CORRECT ANSWER IN THE SPACE AT THE RIGHT.*

1. *"To stand up straight and tread the turning mill,*
   To lie flat and know nothing and be still,
   Are the two trades of man; and which is worse
   I know not, but I know that both are ill."

   In these lines, the one meaning the author does NOT express is that

   A. he does not know whether labor is worse than death
   B. man's fate is only labor and death
   C. man must suffer his labor silently
   D. both labor and death are bad

2. The statement which BEST expresses the meaning of the lines,
   "Only a sweet and virtuous soul,
   Like seasoned timber, never gives," is

   A. The sweet and virtuous are seldom charitable
   B. Only the good and pure in heart attain unyielding strength and fortitude.
   C. Kindly people believe that all people should stand on their own feet.
   D. The sweet and virtuous, disdaining wealth, are like a tree that bears no fruit.

3. In his lines
   "Now Europe balanced, neither side prevails;
   For nothing's left in either of the scales,"
   the author is being

   A. satiric   B. didactic   C. dogmatic   D. cryptic

4. *"The cold drew silver fronds and ferns*
   On every window pane."
   The poetic device employed in the above lines is

   A. onomatopoeia   B. metonymy
   C. personification   D. conceit

5. *"Well, Brutus, thou art noble; yet I see*
   Thy honorable mettle may be wrought
   From that it is disposed."
   The above lines spoken by Cassius are intended to communicate a picture of Brutus as a man whose

   A. patriotism is known to all
   B. honor may not be questioned

C. attitude is not unyielding
D. warlike nature is a danger to Rome

6. *"The white mares of the moon rush along the sky*
   Beating their golden hoofs upon the glass heavens; ..."
   The imagery in the lines above is developed by

   A. extended metaphor
   B. internal rhyme
   C. synecdoche
   D. simile

7. *"Man proposes, God disposes."*
   To juxtapose his ideas in the above statement, the writer has resorted to the use of

   A. hyperbole
   B. antithesis
   C. induction
   D. deduction

Questions 8-14.

DIRECTIONS: Questions 8 through 14 are based on the following passage.

1. ...As in Victorian England, the clowns were still freer than most
2. people; Lewis Carroll and Edward Lear could bring the psyche news it
3. would tolerate only from a jester, and Thurber did the same for us
4. in the puritan twilight of the Depression. The one restriction on
5. such humorists is that they have to tell it. in code -- the more frabjous
6. the better. Carroll's "slithy toves that gire and gimble in the
7. wabe" are like a message from a prison camp. So that's what's going
8. on in there.
9. Thurber's words alone seldom hit quite that kind of black
10. magic, but combined with his pictures they do it repeatedly. Like
11. Disney and later Walt Kelly and Charles Schultz, he produced universal
12. archetypes fit for a T-shirt. But fine as Pogo and Snoopy are, they
13. do not wake you with palms sweating the way Thurber's people do...
14. Thurber was a marvelous comic writer, but alone among such
15. he was able to sketch the phantasmorgoric goo from which his funny
16. ideas came. If Henry James or Dostoevsky had done their own illustra-
17. tions, the results could hardly have been stranger or more illuminating.

8. The author of this passage seems to believe that Thurber's drawings give to his words a(n)

   A. satirical twise
   B. enervating tone
   C. more powerful psychological impact
   D. mollifying effect

9. Edward Lear is BEST known for

   A. ribald tales
   B. sophisticated satire
   C. nonsense verse
   D. mathematical puzzles

10. The phrases "*puritan twilight*" (line 4) and "*phantasmorgic goo*" (line 15) can be classified as

    A. similes B. metaphors C. hyperbole D. litotes

11. The quoted words in lines 6 and 7 could be used by an English teacher to illustrate the importance in the English language of

    A. borrowings from Latin and Greek
    B. word order and inflectional endings
    C. spelling and punctuation
    D. absolute constructions

12. In line 7, that's is underlined to signal the reader

    A. to slow the pace of his reading
    B. that the word is not to be taken seriously
    C. to "hear" that word louder than its surrounding words
    D. that the rest of the sentence is unimportant

13. The words "*hit quite that kind of black magic*" (lines 9-10) might be pointed out by an English teacher as

    A. a mixed metaphor
    B. vulgar slang
    C. improper usage
    D. a proverb

14. In line 12, "*fit for a T-shirt*" implies that the archetypes were

    A. irrelevant to people over 25 years old
    B. relevant chiefly to men and boys
    C. brilliantly colored and less than one square foot in dimension
    D. easily recognizable to a wide audience

15. "*What joy to see, what joy to win
    So fair a land for his kith and kin,
    Of streams unstained and woods unhewn!
    'Elbow room!' laughed Daniel Boone...*"

    According to its use in the poem, the underlined expression means

    A. towering spruce
    B. glades and groves
    C. petrified trees
    D. virgin forests

16. In the quotation from BEOWULF: "*He fain would sail over the swan-road*", swan-road is an example of

    A. alliteration
    B. kenning
    C. scop
    D. colloquy

Questions 17-20.

DIRECTIONS: Questions 17 through 20 are based on the poem quoted below.

> I found a dimpled spider, fat and white
> On a white heal-all, holding up a moth
> Like a white piece of satin cloth–
> Assorted characters of death and blight
> Mixed ready to begin the morning right,
> Like the ingredients of a witches' broth–
> A snow-drop spider, a flower like a froth,
> And dead wings carried like a paper kite.
>
> What had that flower to do with being white,
> The wayside blue and innocent heal-all?
> What brought the kindred spider to that height,
> Then steered the white moth thither in the night?
> What but design of darkness to appall?–
> If design govern in a thing so small.

17. This poem is a

    A. pastoral   B. sonnet   C. lampoon   D. villanelle

18. This poem

    A. poses the problem of evil
    B. argues for the existence of good
    C. finds good in evil
    D. argues against the existence of good

19. A "heal-all" as referred to in the poem is a

    A. medicine   B. moth   C. flower   D. web

20. All the following statements concerning the poem are true EXCEPT:

    A. there are only three rhyme sounds
    B. night, blight, and spider suggest evil
    C. line 5 is ironical
    D. line 1 is an example of hyperbole

KEY (CORRECT ANSWERS)

1. C	6. A	11. B	16. B
2. B	7. B	12. C	17. B
3. A	8. C	13. A	18. A
4. C	9. C	14. D	19. C
5. C	10. B	15. D	20. D

TEST 2

DIRECTIONS: Each question or incomplete statement is followed by several suggested answers or completions. Select the one that BEST answers the question or completes the statement. *PRINT THE LETTER OF THE CORRECT ANSWER IN THE SPACE AT THE RIGHT.*

Questions 1-5.

DIRECTIONS: Questions 1 through 5 are based on the following passage.

1. All morning the climb proceeded, slowly and by easy gradients; but at such height the physical effort was considerable, and none had energy to spare for talk.
2. The Chinese traveled luxuriously in his chair, which might have seemed <u>unchivalrous</u> had it not been absurd to picture Miss Brinklow in such a regal setting.
3. Conway, whom the rarefied air troubled less than the rest, was at pains to catch the occasional chatter of the chairbearers.
4. He knew a very little Tibetan, just enough to gather that the men were glad <u>to be returning to the lamasery</u>.
5. He could not, even has he wished, have continued converse with their leader, since the latter, with eyes closed and face half hidden behind curtains, appeared to have the knack of instant and well-timed sleep.

1. Sentence 1 in this passage is a _____ sentence.
   A. simple
   B. compound
   C. complex
   D. compound-complex

2. The underlined word in Sentence 2 is a(n)
   A. noun
   B. verb
   C. adjective
   D. adverb

3. The subject of Sentence 3 is
   A. air
   B. chatter
   C. chair-bearers
   D. Conway

4. The underlined words in Sentence 4 are an
   A. adjectival phrase
   B. adverbial phrase
   C. adjective clause
   D. adverbial clause

5. The verb of the main clause of Sentence 5 is
   A. could have continued
   B. had wished
   C. closed
   D. appeared

Questions 6-15.

DIRECTIONS: In teaching the poem below, the aim includes not only comprehension of the poem, but also appreciation of poetic structure, interpretation, and use of language. Questions 6 through 15 are based on the poem that follows.

January Chance

1. All afternoon before them, father and boy,
2. In a plush well, with winter sounding past:
3. In the warm cubicle between two high
4. Seat backs that slumber, voyaging the vast.

5. All afternoon to open the deep things
6. That long have waited, suitably unsaid.
7. Now one of them is older, and the other's
8. Art at last has audience; has head,

9. Has heart to take it in. It is the time.
10. Begin, says winter, howling through the pane.
11. Begin, the seat back bumps: what safer hour
12. Than this, within the somnolent loud train,

13. A prison where the corridors slide on
14. As the walls creak, remembering downgrade?
15. Begin. But with a smile that father slumps
16. And sleeps. And so the man is never made.

6. The author's attitude toward the incident depicted in the poem is one of

   A. satisfaction   B. indifference   C. regret   D. envy

7. According to the poem, the deep things

   A. should have been examined long before
   B. were properly and deliberately not discussed
   C. were of no special significance to anyone
   D. were the results of serious disagreements

8. The "*plush well,*" line 2, is an example of a

   A. simile   B. metaphor
   C. personification   D. onomatopoeia

9. The expression "*voyaging the vast,*" line 4, is an example of

   A. onomatopoeia   B. alliteration
   C. simile   D. redundancy

10. The "*other's*" referred to in line 7 is the

    A. boy's   B. warden's   C. audience's   D. father's

11. As used in line 8, "*art*" most probably means skill in

    A. acting   B. painting
    C. using language   D. singing

12. As used in line 8, "*head*" most probably means

    A. handsome features   B. power of comprehension
    C. leadership qualities D. sense of responsibility

13. As used in line 9, "*heart*" most probably means   13.____

    A. violent feeings   B. animation
    C. emotional readiness   D. arrogance

14. The expression "*Begin, says winter,*" line 10, is an example of   14.____

    A. metonomy   B. understatement
    C. personification   D. an invocation

15. The statement below that BEST expresses the *main* idea of the poem is: 15.____

    A. The son failed to take advantage of his father's advice
    B. The father was discouraged from talking to his son by the latter's indifference
    C. The noise of te wind and the train prevented communication between father and son
    D. The father missed an opportunity to help shape his son's future

16. Indicate the use of the underlined words in the stanza below.   16.____

    In Xanadu did Kubla Khan
    A stately <u>pleasure-dome</u> decree:
    Where Alph, the sacred river, ran
    Through caverns measureless to man
    Down to a sunless sea.

    A. subject of <u>ran</u>   B. object of <u>In</u>
    C. subject of <u>did decree</u>   D. object of <u>did decree</u>

Questions 17-20.

DIRECTIONS: Questions 17 through 20 are based on the poem quoted below:

   To one who has been long in city pent,
   'Tis very sweet to look into the fair
   And open face of heaven, -to breathe a prayer
   Full in the smile of the blue firmament.
   Who is more happy, when, with heart's content
   Fatigued he sinks into some pleasant lair
   Of wavy grass, and reads a debonair
   And gentle tale of love and languishment?

   Returning home at evening with an ear
   Catching the notes of Philomel, -an eye
   Watching the sailing cloudlet's bright career,
   He mourns that day so soon has glided by.
   E'en like the passage of an angel's tear
   That falls through the clear ether silently

17. Concerning the poem, all of the following information is true EXCEPT that   17.____

    A. it is a sonnet
    B. the predominant meter is iambic
    C. its rhyme scheme is abba abba cde cde
    D. it is the work of John Keats

18. The poet regrets that

    A. he does not live in the country
    B. the quiet of night is broken by the song of a bird
    C. his day in the country passes so rapidly
    D. his day in the country has fatigued him

19. The poet alludes to the song of the

    A. nightingale   B. thrush   C. swallow   D. whippoorwill

20. In the poem, the poet compares

    A. the sky with a woman's smile
    B. a bird with a tear
    C. a bird with an eye
    D. a day with a tear

KEY (CORRECT ANSWERS)

1.	B	11.	C
2.	C	12.	B
3.	D	13.	C
4.	B	14.	C
5.	A	15.	D
6.	C	16.	D
7.	B	17.	C
8.	B	18.	C
9.	B	19.	A
10.	A	20.	D

TEST 3

DIRECTIONS: Each question or incomplete statement is followed by several suggested answers or completions. Select the one that BEST answers the question or completes the statement. *PRINT THE LETTER OF THE CORRECT ANSWER IN THE SPACE AT THE RIGHT.*

1. The figures of speech illustrated in Yeats' lines,
   "*I will arise and go now, for always night and day,
   I hear lake waters lapping with low sounds by the
        shore,*"
   are

   A. alliteration and metaphor
   B. onomatopoeia and alliteration
   C. onomatopoeia and synecdoche
   D. simile and alliteration

   1.____

2. A mixed metaphor is clearly illustrated in the excerpt,

   A. Out, out, brief candle! Life's but a walking shadow
   B. To feel creep up the curving east the earthly chill of dusk
   C. By the strong lash of tyranny was freedom inundated.
   D. He was a rock to lean on, and yet a frail reed

   2.____

3. "*This is the forest primeval. The murmuring pines and the hemlocks...*"
   The verse form of the above line is

   A. anapestic tetrameter
   B. trochaic hexameter
   C. iambic octameter
   D. dactylic hexameter

   3.____

4. From the far corners of the earth, driven by a deep hunger for freedom, swarmed vast numbers of migrants.
   This sentence is BEST classified in its form as

   A. loose   B. balanced   C. complex   D. periodic

   4.____

Questions 5-9.

DIRECTIONS: Questions 5 through 9 are based on the following passage.

PASSAGE

1. Schiller was the first to ring a change on this state of things
2. by addressing himself courageously to the entire population of his
3. country in all its social strata at one time. He was the great popu-
4. larizer of our theatre, and remained for almost a century the guiding
5. spirit of the German drama of which Schiller's matchless tragedies
6. are still by many people regarded as the surpassing manifestoes.
7. Schiller's position, while it demonstrates a whole people's gratitude
8. to those who respond to its desires, does not however furnish a
9. weapon of self-defense to the "popularizers" of drama, or rather its
10. diluters. Schiller's case rather proves that the power of popular

11. influence wrought upon a poet may be vastly inferior to the strength
12. that radiates from his own personality. Indeed, whereas the secret
13. of ephemeral power is only too often found in paltriness or mediocrity,
14. an influence of enduring force such as Schiller exerts on the Germans
15. can only emanate from a strong and self-assertive character. No poet
16. lives beyond his day who does not exceed the average in mental sta-
17. ture, or who, through a selfish sense of fear of the general, allows
18. himself to be ground down to the conventional size and shape.
19. Schiller, no less than Ibsen, forced his moral demands tyrannically
20. upon his contemporaries. And in the long run your moral despot, pro-
21. vided he be high-minded, vigorous, and able, has a better chance of
22. fame than the pliant time-server. However, there is a great differ-
23. ence between the two cases. For quite apart from the striking dis-
24. similarities between the poets themselves, the public, through the
25. gradual growth of social organization, has become greatly altered.

5. Schiller's lasting popularity may be attributed to

   A. his meeting the desires of a whole people, not just a segment of the people
   B. his abiding by his inmost convictions
   C. his mediocrity and paltriness
   D. his courageous facing up to the problems of his day
   E. his ability to popularize the unknown

6. In the first line, "on this state of things" refers to

   A. romantic drama
   B. the French play of contrived construction
   C. drama directed to the rich and well-born
   D. the popularizers of the theatre of today
   E. the ruling class

7. In the second sentence from the last, "the two cases" refer to

   A. pliant time-server and moral despot
   B. the one who exceeds the average in mental stature and the one who allows himself to be ground down to conventional size
   C. the popularizer and the poet of enduring fame
   D. Ibsen and Schiller
   E. the man of character and the man of wealth

8. We may assume that the author

   A. is no believer in the democratic processes
   B. has no high opinions of the "compact majority"
   C. regards popularity with the people as a measure of enduring success
   D. is opposed to the aristocracy
   E. has no fixed opinions

9. A word used in an ambiguous sense (having 2 or more possible meanings) in this passage is

   A. "poet" (lines 11, 15, 24)
   B. "power" (lines 10, 13)
   C. "people" (lines 6, 7)
   D. "popularizer" (lines 3, 9)
   E. "moral" (lines 19, 20)

Questions 10-13.

DIRECTIONS: Questions 10 through 13 are based on the following passage.

PASSAGE

In one sense, of course, this is not a new insight: all our great social and philosophical thinkers have been keenly aware of the fact of individual differences. It has remained, however, for psychologists to give the insight scientific precision.

What all this adds up to is more than just a working body of information about this and that skill. It adds up to a basic recognition of one important factor in the maturing of the individual. If each individual has a certain uniqueness of power, his maturing will best be accomplished along the line of that power. To try to develop him along lines that go in directions contrary to that of his major strength is to condition him to defeat. Thus, the non-mechanical person who is arbitrarily thrust into a mechanical occupation cannot help but do his work poorly and reluctantly, with some deep part of himself in conscious or unconscious rebellion.

He may blame himself for the low level of his accomplishment or for his persistent discontent; but not all his self-berating, nor even all his efforts to become more competent by further training, can make up for the original aptitude-lack. Unless he discovers his aptitude-lack, he may be doomed to a lifetime of self-blame, with a consequent loss of self-confidence and a halting of his psychological growth.

Or he may take refuge in self-pity—finding reason to believe that his failure is due to one or another bad break, to the jealousy of a superior, to lack of sympathy and help at home, to an initial bad start, to a lack of appreciation of what he does. If he thus goes the way of self-pity, he is doomed to a lifetime of self-commiseration that makes sound growth impossible.

The characteristic of the mature person is that he affirms life. To affirm life he must be involved, heart and soul, in the process of living. Neither the person who feels himself a failure nor the person who consciously or unconsciously resents what life has done to him can feel his heart and soul engaged in the process of living. That experience is reserved for the person whose full powers are enlisted. This, then, is what this fourth insight signifies: to mature, the individual must know what his powers are and must make them competent for life.

10. It is the author's view that

    A. "all men are created equal"
    B. "each man in his life plays many parts"
    C. "all comes to him who waits"

D. "no kernel of nourishing corn can come to one but through his toil bestowed on that plot of ground given to him to till...."
E. "that is what it is not to be alive. To move about in a cloud of ignorance ... to live with envy ... in quiet despair ... to feel oneself sunk into a common grey mass ..."

11. Ignorance of this fourth insight

   A. may very likely cause one to take refuge in self-pity or conscious or unconscious rebellion
   B. constitutes a failure to understand that each individual is different and must cultivate his special powers in socially rewarding ways
   C. is a major deterrent to a growth to maturity
   D. means unawareness of the fact that each must use all his energy and powers to the best of his ability to make him competent for life
   E. may becloud the use of scientific precision

12. Two possible maladjustments of a man thrust into a position he is unfitted for may be summed up in the phrase,

   A. conscious and unconscious rebellion
   B. guilt-feelings and scapegoating
   C. halting of psychological growth and blaming the "breaks"
   D. "Peccavi-I have sinned" and "all the world is made except thee and me and I am not so sure of thee"
   E. light and darkness

13. We will expect a person placed in a job he is unequal to, to

   A. strike out for himself as an extrepreneur
   B. display quick angers and fixed prejudices
   C. show a great love of life outside of his work
   D. engage in labor union activities
   E. join political and social movements

Questions 14-20.

DIRECTIONS: Questions 14 through 20 are based on the following passage.

PASSAGE

1. For the ease and pleasure of treading the old road, accepting
2. the fashions, the education, the religion of society, he takes the
3. cross of making his own, and, of course, the self-accusation, the
4. faint heart, the frequent uncertainty and loss of time, which are the
5. nettles and tangling vines in the way of the self-relying and self-
6. directed; and the state of virtual hositility in which he seems to
7. stand to society, and especially to educated society. For all this
8. loss and scorn, what offset? He is to find consolation in exercising
9. the highest functions of human nature. He is one who raises himself
10. from private consideration and breathes and lives on public and
11. illustrious thoughts. He is the world's eye. He is the world's
12. heart. He is to resist the vulgar prosperity that retrogrades ever

13. to barbarism, by preserving and communicating heroic sentiments,
14. noble biographies, melodious verse, and the conclusions of history.
15. Whatsoever oracles the human heart, in all emergencies, in all solemn
16. hours, has uttered as its commentary on the world of actions – these
17. he shall receive and impart. And whatsoever new verdict Reason from
18. her inviolable seat pronounces on the passing men and events of
19. today – this he shall hear and promulgate.
20. These being his functions, it becomes him to feel all confidence
21. in himself, and to defer never to the popular cry. He and he only
22. knows the world. The world of any moment is the merest appearance.
23. Some great decorum, some fetish of a government, some ephemeral
24. trade, or war, or man, is cried up by half mankind and cried down by
25. the other half, as if all depended on this particular up or down.
26. The odds are that the whole question is not worth the poorest thought
27. which the scholar has lost in listening to the controversy. Let him
28. not quit his belief that a popgun is a popgun, though the ancient and
29. honorable of the earth affirm it to be the crack of doom. In silence,
30. in steadiness, in severe abstraction, let him hold by himself; add
31. observation to observation, patient of neglect, patient of reproach,
32. and bide his own time – happy enough if he can satisfy himself alone
33. that this day he has seen something truly. Success treads on every
34. right step. For the instinct is sure, that prompts him to tell his
35. brother what he thinks. He then learns that in going down into the
36. secrets of his own mind he has descended into the secrets of all
37. minds. He learns that he who has mastered any law in his private
38. thoughts, is master to the extent of all translated. The poet, in
39. utter solitude remembering his spontaneous thoughts and recording
40. them, is found to have recorded that which men in crowded cities
41. find true for them also. The orator distrusts at first the fitness
42. of his frank confessions, his want of knowedge of the persons he
43. addresses, until he finds that he is the complement of his hearers—
44. that they drink his words because he fulfills for them their own
45. nature; the deeper he delves into his privatest, secretest presentiment,
46. to his wonder he finds this is the most acceptable, most public, and
47. universally true. The people delight in it; the better part of every
48. man feels. This is my music; this is myself.

14. It is a frequent criticism of the scholar that he lives by himself, in an "ivory tower," remote from the problems and business of the world. Which of these below constitutes the *BEST* refutation by the writer of the passage to the criticism here noted?   14._____

   A. The world's concern being ephemeral, the scholar does well to renounce them and the world.
   B. The scholar lives in the past to interpret the present.
   C. The scholar at his truest is the spokesman of the people.
   D. The scholar is not concerned with the world's doing because he is not selfish and therefore not engrossed in matters of importance to himself and neighbors.
   E. The scholar's academic researches of today are the businessman's practical products of tomorrow.

15. The scholar's road is rough, according to the passage. Which of these is his GREATEST difficulty?

   A. He must renounce religion.
   B. He must pioneer new approaches.
   C. He must express scorn for, and hostility to, society.
   D. He is uncertain of his course.
   E. There is a pleasure in the main-traveled roads in education, religion, and all social fashions.

16. When the writer speaks of the "world's eye" and the "world's heart," he means

   A. the same thing
   B. culture and conscience
   C. culture and wisdom
   D. a scanning of all the world's geography and a deep sympathy for every living thing
   E. mind and love

17. By the phrase, "nettles and tangling vines," the author PROBABLY refers to

   A. "self-accusation" and "loss of time"
   B. "faint heart" and "self accusation"
   C. "the slings and arrows of outrageous fortune"
   D. a general term for the difficulties of a scholar's life
   E. "self-accusation" and "uncertainty"

18. The various ideas in the passage are BEST summarized in which of these groups?
   1. (a) Truth versus society
      (b) The scholar and books
      (c) The world and the scholar

   2. (a) The ease of living traditionally
      (b) The glory of a scholar's life
      (c) True knowledge versus trivia

   3. (a) The hardships of the scholar
      (b) The scholar's function
      (c) The scholar's justifications for disregarding the world's business

   A. 1 and 3 together
   B. 3 only
   C. 1 and 2 together
   D. 1 only
   E. 1, 2, and 3 together

19. "seems to stand" (lines 6 and 7) means

   A. is
   B. gives the false impression of being
   C. ends probably in becoming
   D. is seen to be
   E. the quicksands of time

20. "public and illustrious thoughts" (lines 10 and 11) means   20._____
    A. what the people think
    B. thoughts for the good of mankind
    C. thoughts in the open
    D. thoughts transmitted by the people
    E. the conclusions of history

KEY (CORRECT ANSWERS)

1. B	11. B
2. C	12. B
3. D	13. B
4. D	14. C
5. B	15. B
6. C	16. C
7. D	17. E
8. B	18. B
9. D	19. B
10. D	20. B

ANALYSIS AND INTERPRETATION OF LITERATURE
EXAMINATION SECTION
TEST 1

DIRECTIONS: The passage below is followed by 10 incomplete statements or questions about the passage. Each question or incomplete statement is followed by several suggested answers or completions. Select the one that BEST answers the question or completes the statement. *PRINT THE LETTER OF THE CORRECT ANSWER IN THE SPACE AT THE RIGHT.*

    Oh, oh, you will be sorry for that word!
    Give back my book and take my kiss instead.
    Was it my enemy or my friend I heard,
    "What a big book for such a little head!"
5   Come, I will show you now my newest hat,
    And you may watch me purse my mouth and prink!
    Oh, I shall love you still, and all of that.
    I never again shall tell you what I think.
    I shall be sweet and crafty, soft and sly;
10 You will not catch me reading any more:
    I shall be called a wife to pattern by;
    And some day when you knock and push the door,
    Some sane day, not too bright and not too stormy,
    I shall be gone, and you may whistle for me.

1. The tone of this poem is

   A. happy   B. sad
   C. indignant   D. amused

1.____

2. What effect does the author achieve by the repetition of "Oh, oh..." in line 1?

   A. It attracts the reader's attention.
   B. It employs the device of onomatopoeia.
   C. It signals the symbol that will follow.
   D. It shows the speaker's shock after hearing "that word."

2.____

3. The implication of line 4, "What a big book for such a little head!" is that

   A. young people should not read lengthy books
   B. women are not bright enough to read significant books
   C. the book is meant for men
   D. the speaker thinks too highly of herself

3.____

4. What change of mood occurs in line 5?

   A. Dismay changes to outward compliance
   B. Acceptance changes to rebellion
   C. Hate changes to love
   D. Enthusiasm changes to despair

4.____

5. What literary device is found in line 9, "I shall be sweet and crafty, soft and sly;"?

   A. Metaphor
   B. Hyperbole
   C. Assonance
   D. Alliteration

6. Lines 8 through 11 suggest that the speaker is

   A. sorry for past actions
   B. developing a strategy for the future
   C. happy about the whole experience
   D. still confused

7. Which statement MOST clearly reflects the implication in lines 12 through 14?

   A. If you whistle for me, I will return.
   B. Some day I will become independent.
   C. When things become dull, I will leave.
   D. I will leave when you want me to.

8. Which line BEST demonstrates the speaker's understanding of the role she is expected to fill?

   A. Line 5
   B. Line 2
   C. Line 7
   D. Line 11

9. Which BEST describes the poetic function of the phrases "some day" and "some sane day" in lines 12 and 13?

   A. The phrases reinforce the rhyme scheme.
   B. The phrases emphasize the indecision of the speaker.
   C. The phrases move from the general to the specific.
   D. The phrases employ figurative language.

10. In line 14, the speaker uses the word "whistle" to suggest that

    A. he has treated her more like a pet than a person
    B. she will not return until he searches for her
    C. she expects him to chase after her
    D. he will still find her attractive

KEY (CORRECT ANSWERS)

1. C
2. D
3. B
4. A
5. D
6. B
7. B
8. D
9. C
10. A

TEST 2

DIRECTIONS: The passage below is followed by 6 incomplete statements or questions about the passage. Each question or incomplete statement is followed by several suggested answers or completions. Select the one that BEST answers the question or completes the statement. *PRINT THE LETTER OF THE CORRECT ANSWER IN THE SPACE AT THE RIGHT.*

      The great city is not necessarily beautiful or well-planned. Venice and Florence are delights to the eye; yet neither has been a great city since the Renaissance. Brasilia, one of the most elaborately designed of modern cities, is
5 also one of the deadliest. An impressive physical setting is essential to a city's greatness, but by itself that is not enough. Take Pittsburgh: its natural setting, at the junction of two rivers, is magnificent. Man botched the job of doing anything with it. Grand avenues and impressive
10 architecture, though necessary to a great city, do not satisfy the equation. If the Third Reich had lasted another ten years, Berlin, which Hitler planned to rename Germania, would have been the most monumentally dull. In fact, it became second-rate on January 30, 1933, when Hitler took
15 power. A city cannot be both great and regimented. Blessed with culture, history and size, Moscow, Shanghai, and Peking ought to be great cities, but they are not. They all lack the most important element: spontaneity of free human exchange. Without that, a city is as sterile as Aristophanes'
20 Nephelococcygia, which was to be suspended between heaven and earth—and ruled by the birds.
      A city governed by birds might be more comfortable than a city governed by men. But it would not be human, nor would it be great; a city is great only in its human associations,
25 confusing as they may be. The ancient Athenians, true urbanites, delighted in the everyday drama of human encounter. For them, the city was the supreme instrument of civilization, the tool that gave its people common traditions and goals, even as it encouraged their diversity and growth.

1. According to this passage, Berlin was not a great city after Hitler took power because it

   A. had too many monuments
   B. was too rigidly organized
   C. was involved in war
   D. had no great architecture

2. According to this passage, which city is impressive because of its size?

   A. Florence   B. Pittsburgh
   C. Peking   D. Berlin

3. According to this passage, one necessary characteristic of a great city is that it
   A. encourages variety
   B. lasts forever
   C. promotes nationalism
   D. ignores growth

4. In line 26, the phrase "everyday drama" is used by the author to
   A. make fun of the Athenians
   B. suggest the tragedies in daily life
   C. emphasize the interaction of people
   D. exaggerate the evils of life

5. In lines 27 and 28, the author uses the words "instrument" and "tool" to suggest that
   A. cities enable people to grow
   B. cities are basic to human life
   C. growth is a planned activity
   D. cities are built for work

6. According to the author, which city can be considered great?
   A. Venice
   B. Brasilia
   C. Pittsburgh
   D. Athens

KEY (CORRECT ANSWERS)

1. B
2. C
3. A
4. C
5. A
6. D

TEST 3

DIRECTIONS: The passage below is followed by 6 incomplete statements or questions about the passage. Each question or incomplete statement is followed by several suggested answers or completions. Select the one that BEST answers the question or completes the statement. *PRINT THE LETTER OF THE CORRECT ANSWER IN THE SPACE AT THE RIGHT.*

My father brought the emigrant bundle
of desperation and worn threads,
that in anxiety as he stumbles
tumble out distractedly;
5   while I am bedded upon soft green money
that grows like grass. Thus,
between my father who lives on a bed of anguish
for his daily bread, and I who tear money
at leisure by the roots,
10   where I lie in sun or shade,
a vast continent of breezes, storms to him,
shadows, darkness to him, small lakes,
difficult channels to him, and hills,
mountains to him, lie between us.

15   My father comes of a hell
where bread and man have been kneaded
and baked together. You have heard the scream
as the knife fell; while I have slept
as guns pounded on the shore.

1. As used in the poem, the expression "soft green money" (line 5) refers to the

   A. narrator's sense of guilt
   B. narrator's life of comparative ease
   C. father's disregard for luxuries
   D. father's "bundle"

2. The narrator's life in America is BEST described by the expression

   A. "money that grows like grass" (lines 5 and 6)
   B. "for his daily bread" (line 8)
   C. "a vast continent of breezes" (line 11)
   D. "while I have slept" (Line 18)

3. The phrase "where I lie in sun or shade" (line 10) implies the narrator is able to

   A. comfort his father
   B. escape from screams
   C. choose his surroundings
   D. ignore unpleasant conditions

4. From the poem the reader can *most likely* conclude that the

   A. narrator wishes to visit Europe
   B. narrator is living the American Dream
   C. father wishes to return to Europe
   D. father is satisfied with his life in America

5. The "hell" referred to in lines 15 through 17 could be expressed as man's

   A. struggle to conquer nature
   B. need to become more sensitive
   C. inability to rise above existing conditions
   D. quest to understand himself

6. Both the title and the content of the poem suggest a

   A. quarrel   B. union
   C. contrast   D. universality

KEY (CORRECT ANSWERS)

1. B
2. A
3. C
4. B
5. C
6. C

TEST 4

DIRECTIONS: The passage below is followed by 7 incomplete statements or questions about the passage. Each question or incomplete statement is followed by several suggested answers or completions. Select the one that BEST answers the question or completes the statement. *PRINT THE LETTER OF THE CORRECT ANSWER IN THE SPACE AT THE RIGHT.*

Since the late 1930s the Bureau of Indian Affairs has been working to promote native language literacy among Indians. Indians were to be taught to read and write in their native language before being taught English. Studies in many
5   cultures around the world demonstrate that children learn to read best in their mother tongue. Bilingual reading books and other educational materials were prepared in Navaho, Hopi, Siouan, Pueblo, and Papago. The difficulties were tremendous because many American Indian languages are distinctively
10 different in structure from all other languages in the world. They are polysynthetic, not analytic. That is, they do not have "words" in the sense that other languages do–as independent meaningful sound sequences that combine into "sentences." Their "sentences" are made by combining prefixes, infixes, and
15 suffixes into what looks like one long word but is essentially the equivalent of our sentence. It is impossible, in other words, to make an Indian utterance that is not a sentence. In our sense, Indian languages do not have parts of speech, conjugations, or declensions. The sentence is the smallest
20 structure available to speakers of the language. Therefore, bridging the translation gap between English and such languages is a massive feat.
    In most cases, Indian children need to be bilingual though not necessarily biliterate. That is, they need to speak their
25 native language to participate fully in their home and tribal affairs, but, unless a literature exists in their native language, they do not need to read and write that language. On the other hand, they also need a reading, writing, and speaking knowledge of English, not only to get their due in this country,
30 but, ironically, also to preserve their heritage.

1. Which phrase BEST expresses the main idea of the passage?   1.____

   A. The importance of bilingual reading books
   B. Historical backgrounds of American-Indian English
   C. The importance of the Bureau of Indian Affairs
   D. Language problems confronting the American Indian

2. Indian bilingual textbooks were difficult to write because   2.____

   A. there were few qualified bilingual writers
   B. there are so many differences among the Indian languages
   C. Indian languages are essentially different in structure from English
   D. Indians were not interested in learning English

3. Indians were taught to read in their native language before being taught to read in English because

   A. English was then learned very easily
   B. some studies show basic literacy is best accomplished through the native language
   C. it is more important for Indians to know their own language than to know English
   D. bilingual textbooks were difficult to write

4. Mistakes that would be impossible to make in the Indian languages are

   A. punctuation errors
   B. spelling errors
   C. sentence fragments
   D. inappropriate word choices

5. According to this passage, the main reason Indians should speak their own language is so that they can

   A. learn to speak English
   B. get their due in the United States
   C. teach their children their literature
   D. maintain their position in their tribe

6. The language concept generally known as a "word" is defined in this passage as

   A. the smallest unit of meaningful sound
   B. a symbol
   C. an idea
   D. a verbal equivalent of a gesture

7. According to this passage, Indians who are literate in English have the advantage of being able to

   A. preserve their own heritage
   B. talk with other English-speaking Indians
   C. better understand United States history
   D. pursue their native literature

KEY (CORRECT ANSWERS)

1. D
2. C
3. B
4. C
5. D
6. A
7. A

TEST 5

DIRECTIONS: The passage below is followed by 7 incomplete statements or questions about the passage. Each question or incomplete statement is followed by several suggested answers or completions. Select the one that BEST answers the question or completes the statement. *PRINT THE LETTER OF THE CORRECT ANSWER IN THE SPACE AT THE RIGHT.*

"But the view is so lovely," my mother said to me. We were standing on the family burial plot, in Pennsylvania. Around us, and sloping down the hill, were the markers of planted farmers. My grandfather's stone, with the family
5   name carved in the form of bent branches, did not seem very much like him. Elsewhere on the plot were his parents, and great-aunts and uncles I had met only at spicy-smelling funerals in my remotest childhood. My mother paced off two yards, saying, "Here's Daddy and me. See how much room is
10 left?"
   "But she"—I didn't have to name my wife—"has never lived here." I was again a child at one of those dreaded family gatherings on dark holiday afternoons—awkward and stuffed and suffocating under the constant need for tact.
15 Only in Pennsylvania, among my kin, am I pressured into such difficult dance-steps of evasion. Every buried coffin was a potential hurt feeling. I tried a perky sideways jig, hopefully humorous, and added, "And the children would feel crowded and keep everybody awake."
20   She turned her face and gazed downward at the view—a lush valley, a whitewashed farmhouse, a straggling orchard, and curved sections of the highway leading to the city whose glistening tip, a television relay, could just be glimpsed five ridges in the distance. She had expected my evasion—
25 but had needed to bring me to it, to breast my refusal and the consequences that, upon receiving her and my father, the plot would be closed, would cease to be a working piece of land. Placatory, I agreed, "The view is lovely."

1. Which phrase BEST expresses the main idea of this passage?

   A. Reality of death
   B. Importance of planning ahead
   C. Importance of life
   D. Role of family tradition

2. The son's evasive attitude is expressed by his

   A. recounting childhood stories
   B. attempt at humor
   C. refusal to discuss the matter
   D. indifference to his mother

3. In the statement, "Here's Daddy and me. See how much room is left?" (line 9), the mother is implying that

   A. she and her husband will be comfortable here
   B. she had planned carefully
   C. her son and his family could also be here
   D. graves cannot be crowded

4. The mother's attitude about her own burial plans can be BEST described as

   A. determined
   B. casual
   C. unsettled
   D. humorous

5. The son's childhood memories of his relatives were

   A. indifferent
   B. unpleasant
   C. dim
   D. fragmentary

6. The son's attitude toward his refusal can be BEST described as

   A. indifferent but wavering
   B. casual and complacent
   C. frustrated and fearful
   D. firm but guilty

7. The ultimate irony about the mother's feelings for the view is that

   A. it is distant from the town
   B. the dead cannot see it
   C. it is typically Pennsylvania
   D. the son does not agree

KEY (CORRECT ANSWERS)

1. D
2. B
3. C
4. A
5. B
6. D
7. B

TEST 6

DIRECTIONS: The passage below is followed by 7 incomplete statements or questions about the passage. Each question or incomplete statement is followed by several suggested answers or completions. Select the one that BEST answers the question or completes the statement. *PRINT THE LETTER OF THE CORRECT ANSWER IN THE SPACE AT THE RIGHT.*

       The theater is a jungle in which the playwright, the actor, and the director struggle for supremacy. Sometimes the fight goes one way and then, for a time, another. I have lived through the reign of each in turn and now it seems to
5   me the playwright is once more supreme. Pinter, Stoppard, and Gray stalk unchallenged by Olivier and Peter Brook. Once more the audience is invited not only to look and listen but to think as they once thought with Shaw and Galsworthy. There is a rich heritage in the British theater, but it is not, alas,
10   the heritage of the actor, still less of the director. The playwright must in the final battle always prove the winner. His work, imperishable; his fame, enduring. I write "alas" because although I have tried my hand at both directing and playwriting, I am in essence one of those of whom Shakespeare
15   wrote that we were destined to strut and fret an hour upon the stage and then be heard no more.
       My generation of actors were trained to entice our prey. We kept an eye open, a claw sharpened, even when we professed to slumber. However deep the tragedy or shallow the farce,
20   we never forgot to face front. Nowadays, the relation between player and public tends to be more sophisticated. Together they share a mutual experience of pain and sorrow. Sometimes the actor seems able to dispense with his audience–to no longer need them. He may choose or chance to perfect his
25   performance on a wet afternoon in Shrewsbury, with hardly anyone watching, and thereafter the repetition for him may stale. For me this never happens. I never perfect a performance, though obviously I am sometimes better or worse, but I have learned that without a perfect audience, my struggle to the
30   summit is impossible. I am aware as the curtain rises of the texture of the house.

1. According to this passage, Pinter, Stoppard, and Gray are involved with the theater as

    A. theater owners   B. actors
    C. playwrights   D. directors

2. Which image is presented in lines 1 through 12?

    A. Producing a play is like a battle
    B. The playwright is like a battle
    C. The director is a hunter who attempts to capture and tame the actors
    D. Actors are like murderers and directors are their victims

3. In lines 12 through 16, what reason does the author give for using the word "alas" in line 9?

    A. He believes that playwrights have too much power
    B. He believes that directors have too much power
    C. He feels he has been ignored
    D. He realizes he has limited abilities

4. What relationship usually exists between the modern actor and his audience?

    A. The actor ignores the audience completely
    B. The actor merely presents the playwright's ideas to the audience
    C. The audience enters into the experience with the actor
    D. The audience must be perfect or the actor will not be successful

5. In lines 17 through 19, the actors of the author's generation are pictured as

    A. hypocrites   B. predators
    C. perfectionists   D. sophisticates

6. The author personally believes that the audience

    A. is vital
    B. is a necessary evil
    C. is largely irrelevant
    D. would rather not think

7. According to this passage, what is the author's usual occupation in the theater?

    A. Playwright   B. Director
    C. Actor   D. Reviewer

KEY (CORRECT ANSWERS)

1. C
2. A
3. D
4. C
5. B
6. A
7. C

TEST 7

DIRECTIONS: The passage below is followed by 7 incomplete statements or questions about the passage. Each question or incomplete statement is followed by several suggested answers or completions. Select the one that BEST answers the question or completes the sentence. *PRINT THE LETTER OF THE CORRECT ANSWER IN THE SPACE AT THE RIGHT.*

My clumsiest dear, whose hands shipwreck vases,
At whose quick touch all glasses chip and ring,
Whose palms are bulls in china, burs in linen,
And have no cunning with any soft thing

5   Except all ill at ease fidgeting people:
The refugee uncertain at the door
You make at home; deftly you steady
The drunk clambering on his undulant floor.

Unpredictable dear, the taxi drivers' terror,
10 Shrinking from far headlights pale as a dime
Yet leaping before red apoplectic streetcars–
Misfit in any space. And never on time.

A wrench in clocks and the solar system. Only
With words and people and love you move at ease.
15 In traffic of wit expertly maneuver
And keep us, all devotion, at your knees.

Forgetting your coffee spreading on our flannel,
Your lipstick grinning on our coat,
So gayly in love's unbreakable heaven
20 Our souls on glory of spilt bourbon float.

Be with me darling early and late. Smash glasses-
I will study wry music for your sake.
For should your hands drop white and empty
All the toys of the world would break.

1. The woman in this poem might be clumsy at washing dishes, but is probably very skillful at

   A. fixing clocks   B. serving coffee
   C. driving a car   D. talking to people

2. The poet's attitude toward the woman in this poem is one of

   A. tolerance   B. disbelief
   C. ridicule   D. endearment

3. The effect of using the words "hands" and "palms" as subjects of the clauses, "whose hands shipwreaked vases" (line 1) and "Whose palms are bulls in china" (line 3), is to

   A. help separate the woman's clumsiness from the woman herself
   B. establish her ineptness
   C. emphasize her great responsibility
   D. make her appear to be ignorant

4. The woman in this poem is the "taxi drivers' terror" (line 9) most likely because she

   A. frightens taxi drivers whenever she rides with them
   B. is an unpredictable pedestrian
   C. is afraid of taxi drivers
   D. jumps off buses

5. The phrase, "For should your hands drop white and empty" (line 23), refers to the woman's

   A. dropping everything
   B. being clumsy
   C. injuring her hands
   D. dying

6. What is the theme of this passage?

   A. Loving others is more important than being graceful
   B. Learning to be on time is important
   C. Clumsy people must be loved despite their faults
   D. Unpredictable people are misfits in society

7. The last line of the poem most likely means

   A. all material things would be destroyed
   B. accidents would occur by themselves
   C. there would be no more joy in the world
   D. his childish entertainment would end

KEY (CORRECT ANSWERS)

1. D
2. D
3. A
4. B
5. D
6. A
7. C

ANALYSIS AND INTERPRETATION OF LITERATURE
EXAMINATION SECTION
TEST 1

DIRECTIONS: The passage below is followed by 10 incomplete statements or questions about the passage. Each question or incomplete statement is followed by several suggested answers or completions. Select the one that BEST answers the question or completes the statement. *PRINT THE LETTER OF THE CORRECT ANSWER IN THE SPACE AT THE RIGHT.*

Filling Out a Blank

High School Profile-Achievement Form

Job Preferences: 1) chemist 2) stage magician
        3) _____

    My preference was to be
    The shrewd man holding up
    A test-tube to the light,
    Or the bowing charlatan
5   Whose inexhaustible hat
    Could fill a stage with birds.
    Lying beyond that,
    Nothing seemed like me.

    Imagining the year
10 In a smock or a frock coat
    Where all was black or white,
    Idly I set about
    To conjure up a man
    In a glare, concocting life
15 Like a rich precipitate
    By acid out of base.

    What shivered up my sleeve
    Was neither rabbit nor gold,
    But a whole bag of tricks:
20 The bubbling of retorts
    In sterile corridors,
    Explosions and handcuffs,
    Time falling through trapdoors
    In a great cloud of smoke,

25 But the third guess leaves me cold:
    It made me draw a blank,
    A stroke drawn with my pen
    Going from left to right
    And fading out of ink

30 As casually as a fact.
    It came to this brief line,
    This disappearing act.

1. In line 3, the phrase, "A test-tube to the light," and in line 23, the phrase, "Time falling through trapdoors," are examples of

   A. alliteration
   B. onomatopoeia
   C. pun
   D. oxymoron

2. The effect of the second stanza is to

   A. explain the speaker's background
   B. present additional choices for the speaker
   C. tell the requirements for each profession
   D. combine elements of two choices

3. Which image helps to unify the first three stanzas?

   A. A test-tube
   B. An inexaustible hat
   C. A bag of tricks
   D. A stage full of birds

4. By denotation, "Where all was black or white" (line 11) refers to the smock or frock coat. By connotation, the line also refers to

   A. moral choices
   B. test-tube and hat
   C. intellectual problems
   D. acid and base

5. Assonance is the repetition of vowel sounds. In this poem, an example of assonance is

   A. "Or the bowing charlatan" (line 4)
   B. "smock or a frock coat" (line 10)
   C. "Explosions and handcuffs" (line 22)
   D. "fading out of ink" (line 29)

6. Which literary technique is used in lines 15 and 16?

   A. Onomatopoeia
   B. Personification
   C. Simile
   D. Understatement

7. The mood at the end of this poem is

   A. optimistic
   B. pessimistic
   C. sarcastic
   D. apathetic

8. The effect of ending this poem with the same images it began with serves to

   A. suggest uncertainty
   B. contrast the symbols
   C. unify the poem
   D. suggest conflicts

9. In the context of the entire poem, the title "Filling Out a Blank" suggests

   A. fulfilling one's roles in life
   B. accepting one's fate
   C. filling a void in one's experiences
   D. completing the form

10. In which poetic form is this poem written?

    A. Spenserian stanzas
    B. Blank verse
    C. Sonnet form
    D. Free verse

KEY (CORRECT ANSWERS)

1. A
2. D
3. C
4. A
5. B

6. C
7. B
8. C
9. A
10. D

TEST 2

DIRECTIONS: The passage below is followed by 6 incomplete statements or questions about the passage. Each question or incomplete statement is followed by several suggested answers or completions. Select the one that BEST answers the question or completes the statement. *PRINT THE LETTER OF THE CORRECT ANSWER IN THE SPACE AT THE RIGHT.*

    She came forward, all in black, with a pale head floating towards me in the dusk. She was in mourning. It was more than a year since his death, more than a year since the news came; she seemed as though she would remember and mourn forever. She took both my hands in hers and murmured, "I had heard you were coming." I noticed she was not very young-I mean not girlish. She had a mature capacity for fidelity, for belief, for suffering. The room seemed to have grown darker, as if all the sad light of the cloudy evening had taken refuge on her forehead. This fair hair, this pale visage, this pure brow, seemed surrounded by an ashy halo from which the dark eyes looked out at me. Their glance was guileless, profound, confident, and trustful. She carried her sorrowful head as though she were proud of that sorrow, as though she would say, "I—I alone know how to mourn him as he deserves." But while we were still shaking hands, such a look of awful desolation came upon her face that I perceived she was one of those creatures that are not the playthings of Time. For her he had died only yesterday.

1. The narrator suggests that the woman appears mature because of her

    A. consciousness of age
    B. acceptance of responsibility
    C. worldly manner
    D. capacity for suffering

2. The woman's forehead seemed to be a resting place for

    A. her inner anxieties
    B. the darkness of the room
    C. the mournful light of the evening
    D. her trust

3. The narrator noticed that the woman appeared especially grief-stricken when

    A. they were shaking hands
    B. he entered the room
    C. he first looked into her eyes
    D. she came forward to greet him

4. When the narrator observes that the woman is not one of the "playthings of Time" (line 12), he probably means that she

    A. is too young to look so old
    B. does not believe in wasting her life
    C. welcomes approaching old age
    D. is not affected by the passage of time

5. The narrator states that the woman will probably grieve for a long time because she

   A. acts as if the man had just died
   B. had known the dead man for a long time
   C. is so very young
   D. is a sensitive person

6. The author's purpose in writing this passage is most probably to

   A. describe the character of the visitor
   B. show the extent of one person's mourning
   C. explain the woman's need for compassion
   D. demonstrate the relationship between the woman and the dead man

KEY (CORRECT ANSWERS)

1. D
2. C
3. A
4. D
5. A
6. B

TEST 3

DIRECTIONS: The passage below is followed by 6 incomplete statements or questions about the passage. Each question or incomplete statement is followed by several suggested answers or completions. Select the one that BEST answers the question or completes the statement. *PRINT THE LETTER OF THE CORRECT ANSWER IN THE SPACE AT THE RIGHT.*

    Sickness is a crime.
        For habitual offenders
            the penalty is death.
    In the doctor's waiting room
5   we study one another
            slyly, like embezzlers.
    In the hospital
        even those who love us
            seem afraid of what
10 we might do to them.
        (The sick have no friends.
           Here there are only strangers,
    brothers and lovers.)
        Anyone who can walk
15   erect without swaying
    is my superior.
        Astonishing how soon
           one learns the tricks
    the weak use
20   against the strong.
        For almost the first time
    I have become
        a credible flatterer. Next
           I will learn to whine
25 - already I find myself
        struggling against it.
           The orderly who sneered
    at the fat bearded man
    in the Mother Hubbard -
30   would I have done differently
    or only been more clever,
        deceiving myself
           that what I felt was pity.

1. In lines 5-6, "we study one another/slyly, like embezzlers," implies that sick people   1.____

   A. sympathize with each other
   B. envy the fate of people who are healthy
   C. are secretly curious to know the illnesses of others
   D. do not really care about other people

2. Which group of words from the poem is the best example of exaggeration?

    A. "Sickness is a crime." (line 1)
    B. "Here there are only strangers," (line 12)
    C. "Anyone who can walk erect without swaying" (lines 14-15)
    D. "I find myself struggling against it." (lines 25-26)

3. In lines 17 through 26, which statement BEST expresses the poet's opinion about sick people?

    A. They ought to be pitied
    B. They want the sympathy of friends and relatives
    C. They dislike having orderlies tend to them
    D. They sometimes take advantage of healthy people

4. Which group of words is used figuratively?

    A. "We study one another slyly, like embezzlers" (lines 5-6)
    B. "Even those who love us seem afraid" (lines 8-9)
    C. "I have become a credible flatterer" (lines 22-23)
    D. "The orderly who sneered" (line 27)

5. The tone of this poem is BEST described as

    A. objective
    B. arrogant
    C. cynical
    D. indifferent

6. The poet's purpose in writing this poem most likely is to

    A. criticize the medical profession
    B. present a picture of the mind of a sick person
    C. condemn the artificiality of hospital visits
    D. present an autobiographical account of his illness

KEY (CORRECT ANSWERS)

1. C
2. A
3. D
4. A
5. C
6. B

TEST 4

DIRECTIONS: The passage below is followed by 7 incomplete statements or questions about the passage. Each question or incomplete statement is followed by several suggested answers or completions. Select the one that BEST answers the question or completes the statement. *PRINT THE LETTER OF THE CORRECT ANSWER IN THE SPACE AT THE RIGHT.*

Those who save money are often accused of loving money; but, in my opinion, those who love money most are those who spend it. To them money is not merely a list of dead figures in a bankbook. It is an animate thing, spasmodically restless like the birds in a wood, taking wings to itself, as the poet has said. Money, to the man who enjoys
5 spending, is the perfect companion - a companion all the dearer because it never outstays its welcome. It is responsive to his every mood.... Age, alas, has blotted out half that world of passionate delight in which I once lived, and to many of the things I once loved I have grown indifferent. The love of money, however, remains. So much do I love it that I feel almost a different person when I have money in my pocket and when I have
10 none. Let me have but money, and, for the time being, I am back among the ardent attachments and illusions of the nursery. From all this I am inclined to conclude that the love of money is a form of infantilism. The man who loves money is the man who has never grown up. He has never passed from the world of fairy tales into the world of philosophy (for philosophy, which is the wisdom of the grown man in contrast to the
15 wonder of the child, is as contemptuous of money as it is of jam, sweets, and bedknobs). Money, according to the philosophers, is dross, filthy lucre, an impediment rather than an aid to true happiness. Those who retain the nursery imagination throughout life, however, cannot be persuaded of this. Money they regard as the loveliest gift ever bestowed on a mortal by the wand of a fairy godmother. They are like boys dreaming of a Treasure
20 Island; and their money-bags become almost as dear to them, as - sometimes, dearer than - their country.

1. According to the first paragraph, money has the quality of

   A. changing a personaltiy   B. causing restlessness
   C. outstaying its welcome   D. inspiring greed

2. During the author's lifetime, many things have changed for him except his

   A. love of money
   B. fear of old age
   C. contempt for philosophy
   D. desire to return to his childhood

3. Which expression in the second paragraph describes the characteristics of men who like money?

   A. "I am inclined to conclude" (line 11)
   B. "the wisdom of the grown man" (lines 14)
   C. "Money...is dross, filthy lucre," (line 16)
   D. "like boys dreaming of a Treasure Island" (lines 19 and 20)

4. The author implies that the "ardent attachments and illusions of the nursery" (lines 10 and 11) include

    A. bankbooks and checkbooks
    B. animals and birds
    C. jams, sweets, and bedknobs
    D. parents and companions

4.____

5. According to the author, philosophers view money as

    A. a throwback to childhood
    B. a necessary evil
    C. a reward for good living
    D. an obstacle to happiness

5.____

6. Some people who love money see its source as

    A. magical   B. destructive
    C. fateful   D. philosophical

6.____

7. In the author's view, the love of money may even compete with

    A. justice   B. patriotism
    C. ambition   D. wisdom

7.____

KEY (CORRECT ANSWERS)

1. A
2. A
3. D
4. C
5. D
6. A
7. B

TEST 5

DIRECTIONS: The passage below is followed by 7 incomplete statements or questions about the passage. Each question or incomplete statement is followed by several suggested answers or completions. Select the one that BEST answers the question or completes the statement. *PRINT THE LETTER OF THE CORRECT ANSWER IN THE SPACE AT THE RIGHT.*

    Mamie beat her head against the bars of a little Indiana town and dreamed of romance and big things off somewhere the way the railroad trains all ran.

5   She could see the smoke of the engines get lost down where the streaks of steel flashed in the sun and when the newspapers came in on the morning mail she knew there was a big Chicago far off, where all the trains ran.

    She got tired of the barber shop boys and the post office chatter and the church gossip and the old pieces the band played on the
10   Fourth of July and Decoration Day

    And sobbed at her fate and beat her head against the bars and was going to kill herself

    When the thought came to her that if she was going to die she might as well die struggling for a clutch of romance among the streets
15   of Chicago.

    She has a job now at six dollars a week in the basement of the Boston Store

    And even now she beats her head against the bars in the same old way and wonders if there is a bigger place the railroads run to
20   from Chicago where maybe there is

        romance
        and big things
        and real dreams
        that never go smash.

1. What do the "bars" in line 1 symbolize?

    A. A way of showing how small Mamie's town is.
    B. The moral conventions of a small town life.
    C. A contrast of hope and fear.
    D. Mamie's feeling of being trapped.

2. The words "chatter" in line 8 and "gossip" in line 9 both indicate that

    A. the people had nothing to do
    B. conversation in Mamie's town is limited
    C. Mamie liked to talk to people
    D. people got excited over bad news

3. Which phrase BEST expresses Mamie's attitude toward her town?

   A. "the morning mail" (line 6)
   B. "where all the trains ran" (line 7)
   C. "the barber shop boys" (line 8)
   D. "a clutch of romance" (line 14)

4. Which expression is an example of figurative language?

   A. "beat her head against the bars" (line 1)
   B. "Where all the trains ran" (line 7)
   C. "The post office chatter" (line 8)
   D. "If she was going to die" (line 13)

5. In which line is there a definite shift in the tone of the poem?

   A. Line 8   B. Line 11   C. Line 16   D. Line 22

6. Mamie's lack of success in finding romance in Chicago is indicated by the word

   A. "dollars" (line 16)
   B. "basement" (line 16)
   C. "dreams" (line 23)
   D. "smash" (line 24)

7. The poem suggests that if Mamie were to go somewhere other than Chicago, her dreams would

   A. not be fulfilled
   B. most likely come true
   C. reflect her homesickness
   D. become more realistic

KEY (CORRECT ANSWERS)

1. D
2. B
3. C
4. A
5. C
6. D
7. A

TEST 6

DIRECTIONS: The passage below is followed by 7 incomplete statements or questions about the passage. Each question or incomplete statement is followed by several suggested answers or completions. Select the one that BEST answers the question or completes the statement. *PRINT THE LETTER OF THE CORRECT ANSWER IN THE SPACE AT THE RIGHT.*

The football is oval in shape, usually thrown in a spiral, and when kicked end over end may prove difficult to catch. If not caught on the fly, it bounces around eratically.
   The apparent intent of the game is to deposit the ball across the
5 oponent's goal line. Any child with a ball of his own might do it, six days a week and most of Sunday morning, but the rules of the game specify it must be done with members of both teams present and on the field. Owing to large-scale substitutions this is often difficult.
10   In the old days people went crazy trying to follow the ball. The players still do, but the viewing public, who are watching the game on TV, can relax and wait for the replay. If anything happens, that's where you'll see it. The disentanglement of bodies on the goal line is one of the finer visual moments available to sports
15 fans. The tight knot bursts open, the arms and legs miraculously return to the point of rest, before the ball is snapped. Some find it unsettling. Is this what it means to be born again?
   All ball games feature hitting and socking, chopping and slicing, smashing, slamming, stroking, and whacking, but only in football
20 are these blows diverted from the ball to the opponent. And the more the players are helped or carried from the field, the more attendance soars. This truly male game is also enjoyed by women who find group therapy less rewarding. The sacking of the passer by the front four is especially gratifying. Charges that a criminal
25 element threatens the game are a characteristic, but hopeful, exaggeration. What to do with big, mean, boyish-hearted men, long accustomed to horsing around in good clean dormitories, unaccustomed to the rigors of life in the Alaska oilfields, was, until football, a serious national dilemma.

1. Which audience would most likely find the greatest enjoyment in this passage?   1.___

   A. Young boys who plan to play football
   B. Women who love sports
   C. Nonathletic Americans
   D. Professional football players

2. The purpose of the second paragraph is to suggest that football   2.___

   A. has very strict rules
   B. is a simple game made unnecessarily complicated
   C. can be played anywhere and anytime
   D. is best played on a regulation field

3. According to the passage, football is unlike other sports in that it

   A. is played with a ball which is difficult to catch
   B. is being infiltrated by criminals
   C. relies on instant replay as a vital part of the game
   D. directs violence at the players rather than at the ball

4. The author of this passage most likely believes that

   A. football is overrated
   B. most women want to play football
   C. sports are to be played rather than watched
   D. too many injuries occur in football

5. One of the ironies of football is that

   A. the players cannot follow the ball as well as the viewers
   B. children can play the game
   C. the game is played by men acting like children
   D. both men and women love the game

6. The author describes the football players as

   A. lovers of violence
   B. overgrown boys
   C. members of organized crime
   D. oilfield workers

7. The tone of this passage can BEST be described as

   A. argumentative   B. questioning
   C. suspenseful   D. satiric

KEY (CORRECT ANSWERS)

1. C
2. B
3. D
4. A
5. A
6. B
7. D

TEST 7

DIRECTIONS: The passage below is followed by 7 incomplete statements or questions about the passage. Each question or incomplete statement is followed by several suggested answers or completions. Select the one that BEST answers the question or completes the statement. *PRINT THE LETTER OF THE CORRECT ANSWER IN THE SPACE AT THE RIGHT.*

The Whipping

The old woman across the way
   is whipping the boy again
and shouting to the neighborhood
   her goodness and his wrongs.

5   Wildly he crashes through elephant ears,
   pleads in dusty zinnias,
while she in spite of crippling fat
   pursues and corners him.

She strikes and strikes the shrilly circling
10   boy till the stick breaks
in her hand. His tears are rainy weather
   to woundlike memories:

My head gripped in bony vise
   of knees, writhing struggle
15   to wrench free, the blows, the fear
   worse than blows that hateful

Words could bring, the face that I
   no longer knew or loved...
Well, it is over now, it is over,
20   and the boy sobs in his room,

And the woman leans muttering against
   a tree, exhausted, purged -
avenged in part for lifelong hidings
   she has had to bear.

1. The whipping occurs in a

   A. garden   B. street   C. driveway   D. bedroom

2. The poet views the whipping as

   A. an unusual punishment for the boy
   B. inappropriate punishment for the boy
   C. acceptable as a punishment for the boy
   D. helpful in correcting the boy's errors

3. From lines 13 through 15, it is evident that the 3.____

   A. boy in the poem was fighting to get away
   B. poet had also suffered beatings
   C. old woman held the boy's head between her knees
   D. boy's head was held in a vise

4. In lines 17 and 18, the poet "no longer knew or loved" the face because it most likely 4.____

   A. had become a strange face to him
   B. had aged suddenly
   C. was twisted with age
   D. was the face of a criminal

5. In the final stanza, the woman feels cleansed because she has 5.____

   A. released her own frustrations
   B. done her duty in punishing the boy
   C. tired herself out
   D. succeeded in catching the boy

6. In lines 21 through 24, the poet's attitude toward the woman is one of 6.____

   A. spitefulness   B. indifference
   C. fear   D. understanding

7. Lines 23 and 24 suggest that the woman has 7.____

   A. an easy life
   B. sympathy for the boy
   C. unpleasant memories
   D. a deep hatred for the boy

KEY (CORRECT ANSWERS)

1. A
2. B
3. B
4. C
5. A
6. D
7. C

ANALYSIS AND INTERPRETATION OF LITERATURE
EXAMINATION SECTION
TEST 1

DIRECTIONS: The passage below is followed by 10 incomplete statements or questions about the passage. Each question or incomplete statement is followed by several suggested answers or completions. Select the one that BEST answers the question or completes the statement. *PRINT THE LETTER OF THE CORRECT ANSWER IN THE SPACE AT THE RIGHT.*

How is one to speak of the illness of a city? A clear day can come, a morning in early May like the pride of June. The streets are cool, the buildings have come out of shadow, and silences are broken by the voices of children. It is as if the neighborhood has
5 slept in the winding street of the past. Forty years go by—one can recollect the milkman and the clop of a horse. It is a great city. Everyone speaks of the delight of the day on the way to work. It is hard, on such mornings to believe that New York is the victim "etherized on a table."
10 Yet by afternoon the city is incarcerated once more. Haze covers the sky, a grim, formless glare blazes back from the horizon. The city has become unbalanced again. By the time work is done, New Yorkers push through the acrid lung-rotting air and work their way home, avoiding each other's eyes in the subways. Later, near mid-
15 night, thinking of a walk to buy the TIMES, they hesitate—in the darkness a familiar sense of dread returns, the streets are not quite safe, the sense of waiting for some apocalyptic fire, some night of long knives hangs over the city. We recognize one more time that the city is ill, that our own New York, the empire city, is not too
20 far from death.
Recollect: When we were children, we were told air was invisible, and it was. Now we see it shift and thicken, move in gray depression over a stricken sky. Now we grow used to living with colds all year, and viruses suggestive of plague. Tempers shorten in our hideous
25 air. The sick get sicker, the violent more violent. The frayed tissue of New York manners seems ready to splatter on every city street.

1. The organization of the passage follows the cycle of

    A. past, present, and future B. a day
    C. a week   D. the seasons

2. The mood of the passage as a whole is one of

    A. apathy   B. confusion
    C. resignation D. despair

3. The passage concludes on a note of

    A. rising frustration   B. light irony
    C. partial acceptance   D. political rebellion

4. Which figure of speech is illustrated in lines 4 and 5 by the phrase "the neighborhood has slept in the winding street of the past?"

   A. Exaggeration
   B. Personification
   C. Simile
   D. Alliteration

5. In line 10, the city is incarcerated by the

   A. "shadow" (line 3)
   B. "afternoon" (line 10)
   C. "haze" (line 10)
   D. "sense of dread" (line 16)

6. Which phrase is consistent with the descriptive word choices throughout the passage?

   A. Screaming sirens
   B. Disease-ridden
   C. Speed kills
   D. Foul weather

7. The colorful appeal of the passage results mostly from

   A. connective words
   B. repeated idioms
   C. figurative language
   D. parallel sentence structure

8. In line 17, the phrase "apocalyptic fire" and in lines 18 and 19, the phrase "night of long knives hangs over the city" suggest

   A. an imminent threat to the city
   B. the present anarchy in the city
   C. the eventual danger to the city
   D. an imminent invasion by an enemy

9. The effect of the metaphor in lines 22 and 23 is one of

   A. suffocation
   B. nostalgia
   C. wonder
   D. anger

10. Which lines makes the MOST, dramatic use of repetition?

    A. Lines 1-5
    B. Lines 6-9
    C. Lines 10-12
    D. Lines 24-25

KEY (CORRECT ANSWERS)

1. B
2. D
3. A
4. B
5. C
6. B
7. C
8. A
9. A
10. D

TEST 2

DIRECTIONS: The passage below is followed by 6 incomplete statements or questions about the passage. Each question or incomplete statement is followed by several suggested answers or completions. Select the one that BEST answers the question or completes the statement. *PRINT THE LETTER OF THE CORRECT ANSWER IN THE SPACE AT THE RIGHT.*

      She walked along the river until a policeman stopped her. It was one o'clock, he said. Not the best time to be walking alone by the side of a half-frozen river. He smiled at her, then offered to walk her home. It was the first day of the new year, 1946, eight
5 and a half months after the British tanks had rumbled into Bergen-Belsen.
      That February, my mother turned twenty-six. It was difficult for strangers to believe that she had ever been a concentration camp inmate. Her face was smooth and round. She wore lipstick
10 and applied mascara to her large dark eyes. She dressed fashionably. But when she looked into the mirror in the mornings before leaving for work, my mother saw a shell, a mannequin who moved and spoke but who bore only a superficial resemblance to her real self. The people closest to her had vanished. She had no proof that they
15 were truly dead. No eyewitnesses had survived to vouch for her husband's death. There was no one living who had seen her parents die. The lack of confirmation haunted her. At night before she went to sleep and during the day as she stood pinning dresses she wondered if, by some chance, her parents had gotten past the Germans or had
20 crawled out of the mass grave into which they had been shot and were living, old and helpless, somewhere in Poland. What if only one of them had died? What if they had survived and had died of cold or hunger after she had been liberated, while she was in Celle dancing with British officers?
25   She did not talk to anyone about these things. No one, she thought, wanted to hear them. She woke up in the mornings, went to work, bought groceries, went to the Jewish Community Center and to the housing office like a robot.

1. The policeman stopped the author's mother from walking along the river because   1._____

   A. the river was dangerous
   B. it was the wrong time of day
   C. it was still wartime
   D. it was too cold

2. The author states that her mother thought about her parents when she   2._____

   A. walked along the river
   B. thought about death
   C. danced with the officers
   D. was at work

3. When the author mentions her mother's dancing with British officers, she implies that her mother

    A. compared her dancing to the suffering of her parents
    B. had clearly put her troubles behind her
    C. felt it was her duty to dance with them
    D. felt guilty about dancing

4. The mother did not discuss her concerns about her loved ones with anyone because she

    A. thought no one was interested
    B. felt it was no one's business
    C. was too shy
    D. did not know anyone

5. The author's ability to detail her mother's thoughts suggests that the author

    A. has lived through the same experience
    B. has antiwar sentiments
    C. is sympathetic and attentive
    D. is religious and thoughtful

6. The author's purpose in writing this passage is most likely to

    A. inform people about atrocities in the concentration camp
    B. explain the long-range effects of a traumatic experience
    C. enlist active participation in refugee affairs
    D. encourage people to prosecute former concentration camp guards

---

KEY (CORRECT ANSWERS)

1. B
2. D
3. D
4. A
5. C
6. B

TEST 3

DIRECTIONS: The passage below is followed by 6 incomplete statements or questions about the passage. Each question or incomplete statement is followed by several suggested answers or completions. Select the one that BEST answers the question or completes the statement. *PRINT THE LETTER OF THE CORRECT ANSWER IN THE SPACE AT THE RIGHT.*

    Lie back, daughter, let your head
    be tipped back in the cup of my hand.
    Gently, and I will hold you. Spread
    your arms wide, lie out on the stream
5 and look high at the gulls. A dead-
    man's float is face down. You will dive
    and swim soon enough where this tidewater
    ebbs to the sea. Daughter, believe
    me, when you tire on the long thrash
10 to your island, lie up, and survive.
    As you float now, where I held you
    and let you go, remembering when fear
    cramps your heart, what I told you:
    lie gently and wide to the light-year
15 stars, lie back, and the sea will hold you.

1. The statement "Spread your arms wide, lie out on the stream and look high at the gulls" (lines 3 through 5) suggests that the father

    A. understands that his daughter can now float
    B. realizes that his daughter does not fear the water
    C. need not teach his daughter any longer
    D. asks his daughter to gain self-confidence

1.____

2. The statement "You will dive and swim soon enough" (lines 6 and 7) most likely indicates that the father

    A. resents the daughter's impatience
    B. looks forward to the daughter swimming alone
    C. imagines the daughter facing life alone
    D. will teach the daughter diving and swimming

2.____

3. By saying "Daughter, belive me" (lines 8 and 9), the father is really of fering her his

    A. warning   B. support
    C. fear   D. philosophy

3.____

4. By saying to his daughter "when you tire on the long thrash to your island, lie up, and survive" (lines 9 and 10), the father most likely means a time when she

    A. is floundering in deep water
    B. feels discouraged
    C. suffers pain
    D. needs to be alone

4.____

5. In line 10, the word "island" symbolizes a

   A. goal
   B. dream
   C. rejection
   D. new home

6. The father's final advice to his daughter (lines 14 and 15) may be summed up as

   A. float through life
   B. avoid fearful situations
   C. trust both yourself and life
   D. be open to all experiences

KEY (CORRECT ANSWERS)

1. D
2. C
3. D
4. B
5. A
6. C

TEST 4

DIRECTIONS: The passage below is followed by 7 incomplete statements or questions about the passage. Each question or incomplete statement is followed by several suggested answers or completions. Select the one that BEST answers the question or completes the statement. *PRINT THE LETTER OF THE CORRECT ANSWER IN THE SPACE AT THE RIGHT.*

I turned on my back and floated, looking up at the sky, nothing around me but cool clear Pacific, nothing in my eyes but long blue space. It was as close as I ever got to cleanliness and freedom, as far as I ever got from all the people. They had jerry-
5 built the beaches from San Diego to the Golden Gate, bulldozed superhighways through the mountains, cut down a thousand years of redwood growth, and built an urban wilderness in the desert. They couldn't touch the ocean. They poured their sewage into it, but it couldn't be tainted.
10 There was nothing wrong with Southern California that a rise in the ocean level wouldn't cure. The sky was flat and empty, and the water was chilling me. I swam to the kelp-bed and plunged down through it. It was cold and clammy like the bowels of fear. I came up gasping and sprinted to shore with a barracuda terror nipping at
15 my heels.
I was still chilly a half-hour later, crossing the pass to Nopal Valley. Even at its summit, the highway was wide and new, rebuilt with somebody's money. I could smell the source of the money when I slid down into the valley on the other side. It stank like rotten
20 eggs.
The oil wells from which the sulphur gas rose crowded the slopes on both sides of the town. I could see them from the highways as I drove in: the latticed triangles of the derricks where trees had grown, the oil-pumps nodding and clanking where cattle had grazed.
25 Since 'thirty-nine or 'forty, when I had seen it last, the town had grown enormously, like a tumor.

1. In the first paragraph, the ocean is the symbol of nature's

   A. inability to adapt
   B. resistance to humanity's endeavors
   C. submission to a mechanized society
   D. attack on technology

   1.____

2. What is the narrator's attitude toward people as expressed in the first paragraph?

   A. They are like the cool clear Pacific
   B. He is indifferent toward them
   C. Nature is nothing without them
   D. Freedom is preferable to an association with them

   2.____

3. The tone of lines 9 and 10 can BEST be described as

   A. sarcastic
   B. optimistic
   C. nostalgic
   D. cautious

   3.____

4. What are the prevailing images in lines 10 through 14?

   A. Light and dark
   B. Cold and heat
   C. Terror and fear
   D. Death and defeat

5. In this passage, the narrator apparently is trying to

   A. appeal to legislators for environmental action
   B. inform readers of what Southern California looks like
   C. indicate his disapproval of what has been done
   D. show the potential beauty of the area

6. In the last paragraph, the main idea is developed through the use of

   A. cause and effect
   B. contrast
   C. analogy
   D. incident

7. In the last paragraph, the narrator feels that the growth of the town is

   A. detrimental
   B. inevitable
   C. progressive
   D. hasty

KEY (CORRECT ANSWERS)

1. B
2. D
3. A
4. C
5. C
6. B
7. A

TEST 5

DIRECTIONS: The passage below is followed by 7 incomplete statements or questions about the passage. Each question or incomplete statement is followed by several suggested answers or completions. Select the one that BEST answers the question or completes the statement. *PRINT THE LETTER OF THE CORRECT ANSWER IN THE SPACE AT THE RIGHT.*

      In the archives of Smith College's Library there exists a delightful letter from George Washington Cable to his friend, Harry Norman Gardiner. "Dear Mr. Gardiner," the letter begins, "Will you go fishing again this afternoon to the same place, the
5 watery graveyard of the oarlock and the rod-tip? You will have only your own equipment to provide and we will take a basket of lunch along, and stay to our heart's content, and come home to a fresh bite spread just for us. And there will be the fruit of the vine in the basket, and we will angle for that pickerel....O Come,
10 come away! When shall we start?"
      This genteel and lyrical invitation, dated July 13, 1901, shows just how far we've drifted from the simple joys of fishing. I mean, of course, the unspeakable rod-and-gun columns and magazines, the big money "pro-am fishout" contests to catch the biggest fish, and
15 the lure-of-the-month mentality, all of which have threatened in recent years to transform fishing from a Tom Sawyer expedition to a NATO maneuver.
      In a sense, fishing, which is by very far the most popular sport in the country, has become a kind of subsidiary enterprise of
20 the great propaganda machines that sell war, sex, and automobile technology to the American male and his adolescent sons. The fish is no longer incidental to the experience of fishing, nor to the friendship of a Cable for a Gardiner.
      No, the fish has become an enemy, still another threat to our
25 self-image, to be pursued, subdued, and vanquished. It's the awful way of our culture to swamp every activity with volumes of complicating instruction which keep us from feeling true emotion. We are losing the right to say, as Hemingway does in BIG TWO-HEARTED RIVER, "Nick's heart tightened as the trout moved. He felt all the old
30 feeling."

1. Which statement BEST expresses the main idea of this passage?

    A. Fishing is the most popular sport in the United States.
    B. Fishing has been changed by advertising interests.
    C. Fishing no longer unites friends.
    D. Fishing is essential for survival.

2. The author's attitude toward the letter from Cable to Gardiner can BEST be described as

    A. admiring   B. amused
    C. bored   D. flippant

3. In line 13, the word "unspeakable" reveals the author's attitude toward

   A. fishermen
   B. modern sports
   C. NATO maneuvers
   D. sports propaganda

4. In lines 18 through 23, the reader can infer that the author's attitude toward modern-day fishing is

   A. concerned
   B. critical
   C. interested
   D. indifferent

5. In line 20, the phrase "the great propaganda machines" refers to the

   A. mass media
   B. Federal Government
   C. fishing industry
   D. automobile industry

6. In lines 23 and 24, the author implies that the fish has become the enemy because

   A. people no longer like to fish
   B. fish have learned to outwit people
   C. fishing has become a symbol of mastery
   D. fishing has too many regulations

7. The author's main purpose in writing this passage most likely is to

   A. train fishermen
   B. entertain with tales of the past
   C. promote the fishing industry
   D. mourn the passing of simple joys

KEY (CORRECT ANSWERS)

1. B
2. A
3. D
4. B
5. A
6. C
7. D

TEST 6

DIRECTIONS: The passage below is followed by 7 incomplete statements or questions about the passage. Each question or incomplete statement is followed by several suggested answers or completions. Select the one that BEST answers the question or completes the statement. *PRINT THE LETTER OF THE CORRECT ANSWER IN THE SPACE AT THE RIGHT.*

America

Although she feeds me bread of bitterness
And sinks into my throat her tiger's tooth,
Stealing my breath of life, I will confess
I love this cultured hell that tests my youth !
5 Her vigor flows like tides into my blood,
Giving me strength erect against her hate.
Her bigness sweeps my being like a flood.
Yet as a rebel fronts a king in state,
I stand within her walls with not a shred
10 Of terror, malice, not a word of jeer.
Darkly I gaze into the days ahead,
And see her might and granite wonders there,
Beneath the touch of Time's unerring hand,
Like priceless treasures sinking in the sand.

1. Lines 9 and 10 imply that the poet is

   A. frightened and nervous
   B. proud and revengeful
   C. calm and self-contained
   D. angry and defiant

2. Which quote from this poem is NOT an example of figurative language?

   A. "bread and bitterness" (line 1)
   B. "tiger's tooth" (line 2)
   C. "like tides" (line 5)
   D. "days ahead" (line 11)

3. The poet expresses his feeling toward America as one of

   A. love   B. malice
   C. terror   D. indifference

4. Which group of words most vividly uses exaggeration for effect?

   A. "she feeds me bread of bitterness" (line 1)
   B. "sinks into my throat her tiger's tooth" (line 2)
   C. "I will confess" (line 3)
   D. "her might and granite wonders" (line 12)

5. The poet views the greatest of all forces as

   A. America
   B. the tides
   C. time
   D. civilization

6. The poet expresses a paradox in stating that America both

   A. flows and ebbs
   B. rebels and rules
   C. nourishes and destroys
   D. grows and dies

7. The poet views his relationship with America as one of

   A. child and parent
   B. prisoner and warden
   C. pupil and teacher
   D. rebel and authority

KEY (CORRECT ANSWERS)

1. C
2. D
3. A
4. B
5. C
6. C
7. D

TEST 7

DIRECTIONS: The passage below is followed by 7 incomplete statements or questions about the passage. Each question or incomplete statement is followed by several suggested answers or completions. Select the one that BEST answers the question or completes the statement. *PRINT THE LETTER OF THE CORRECT ANSWER IN THE SPACE AT THE RIGHT.*

Some new religious groups answer the need young people feel today for a way of life not based on accumulation and competition. Others promise an experience of the holy, undiluted by the accommodations Christianity and Judaism have made to consumer culture.
5 Thus, minority religious movements can also be seen as symptoms of a hunger seemingly too deep for our existing religious institutions to feed.
   I doubt if many people will ultimately find answers in these movements. Most of those who try an Oriental path will eventually
10 find it too exotic for the Western psyche. They will then turn, as some are doing already, to the neglected spiritual and critical dimensions of our own traditions. Meanwhile, minority movements need protection, in part because they help us to see what is missing in our own way of life.
15   American culture has an enormous capacity to domesticate its critics. It is not unique in that respect. Christianity was once an exotic cult, providing a way of life visibly different from the jaded society around it. After a short period of persecution, it accommodated to the culture so well it was eventually accepted as
20 Rome's only legitimate religion. Christians then quickly turned to the persecution of other religions. The same thing could happen to today's "cultists."
   A new test of America's capacity for genuine pluralism is under way. We could flank it by driving unconventional religious move-
25 ments into accommodation before their message can be heard. It is important to preserve freedom of religion, not only for the sake of the minority immediately involved but also because the majority needs to hear what the minority is saying.

1. The purpose of the first paragraph is to

   A. present reasons for the existence of religions
   B. explain the rise of minority religious movements
   C. suggest how major religions can survive
   D. criticize the increasing popularity of cults

2. According to this passage, young people will not be satisfied by minority Oriental religious movements because those movements contain beliefs that will

   A. ultimately seem too foreign
   B. be as prejudicial as major religions
   C. soon become commonplace
   D. neglect important traditions

1.____

2.____

3. According to this passage, those people who try Oriental religions will later

   A. drop all religious beliefs
   B. start American cults
   C. turn to traditional Western religions
   D. protect minority religions

4. According to the authors, in its early days, Christianity was an

   A. escape from a corrupt way of life
   B. answer to the demands of a complex society
   C. intermingling of two different cultures
   D. offshoot of the popular beliefs

5. The authors support the existence of minority religious movements primarily because they

   A. are protected by the Constitution
   B. help fight immorality
   C. eventually become major religions
   D. provide varied points of view

6. The predominant tone of this passage is

   A. hostile   B. passive
   C. objective   D. pessimistic

7. Which statement BEST expresses the main idea of this passage?

   A. Young people need new religions.
   B. Religious freedom is essential.
   C. Cults can be dangerous.
   D. Minority religious movements are not the answer.

KEY (CORRECT ANSWERS)

1. B
2. A
3. C
4. A
5. D
6. C
7. B

ANALYSIS AND INTERPRETATION OF LITERATURE
EXAMINATION SECTION
TEST 1

DIRECTIONS: The passage below is followed by 4 incomplete statements or questions about the passage. Each question or incomplete statement is followed by several suggested answers or completions. Select the one that BEST answers the question or completes the statement. *PRINT THE LETTER OF THE CORRECT ANSWER IN THE SPACE AT THE RIGHT.*

> Stop all the clocks, cut off the telephone,
> Prevent the dog from barking with a juicy bone,
> Silence the pianos and with muffled drum
> Bring out the coffin, let the mourners come.
>
> 5 Let aeroplanes circle moaning overhead
> Scribbling on the sky the message He Is Dead,
> Put crepe bows round the white necks of the public doves,
> Let the traffic policemen wear black cotton gloves.
>
> He was my North, my South, my East, my West,
> 10 My working week, and my Sunday rest,
> My noon, my midnight, my talk, my song:
> I thought that love would last for ever: I was wrong.
>
> The stars are not wanted now; put out every one:
> Pack up the moon and dismantle the sun;
> 15 Pour away the ocean and sweep up the woods;
> For nothing now can ever come to any good.

1. In line 1, the effect of using the one-syllable words "stop" and "cut" is to

   A. hide the speaker's grief completely
   B. create an instant picture for the reader
   C. fill the reader with similar suffering
   D. emphasize the shock the speaker has suffered

2. In line 2, the poet describes the bone as "juicy" in order to suggest that the dog will

   A. bark again soon
   B. remain quiet for a long time
   C. obey his master
   D. bark more loudly next time

3. In line 6, which poetic device is used in the phrase "Scribbling on the sky"?

   A. Onomatopoeia   B. Pun
   C. Alliteration   D. Simile

4. Which statement BEST summarizes the third Stanza?
   A. He was everything to me, but I lost him.
   B. He was with me everywhere I went.
   C. He was always talking or singing.
   D. He was my life, my everything.

KEY (CORRECT ANSWERS)

1. D
2. B
3. C
4. A

TEST 2

DIRECTIONS: The passage below is followed by 6 incomplete statements or questions about the passage. Each question or incomplete statement is followed by several suggested answers or completions. Select the one that BEST answers the question or completes the statement. *PRINT THE LETTER OF THE CORRECT ANSWER IN THE SPACE AT THE RIGHT.*

The madness grew from week to week, With every revolution of
the clock, the Chaos of the Cultures grew. But through it all
the soul of Dr. Turner kept its feet. Turner hewed true and took
the Middle Way. To all things in their course, in their true
5   proportion, he was just.
    True, he had lapses. In culture's armies he was not always
foremost to the front. But he caught up. He always caught up.
If there were sometimes errors in his calculations, he always rectified them before it was too late. If he made mistakes—like
10   the man he was, he gallantly forgot them.
    It was inspiring just to watch his growth. In 1923, for
instance, he referred to ULYSSES of James Joyce as "that encyclopedia of filth which has become the bible of our younger intellectuals which differs from the real one in that it manages to be so consis-
15   tently dull;" in 1929 (behold this man!) as "that amazing tour de
force which has had more influence on our younger writers than any
other work or our generation;" and in 1933, when Justice Woolsey
handed down the famous decision that made the sale of ULYSSES
legally permissible throughout these United States (in a notable
20   editorial that covered the entire front page of the FORTNIGHTLY
CYCLE)., as "a most magnificent vindication of artistic integrity...
the most notable triumph over the forces of bigotry and intolerance
that has been scored in the Republic of Letters in our time."

1. The statement, "In culture's armies he was not always foremost to the front" (line 6) indicates that Dr. Turner   1.____

   A. was never swayed by public opinion
   B. fought to preserve old values
   C. was sometimes slow to recognize change
   D. had his own unique ideas

2. Which statement does the author make about Dr. Turner?   2.____

   A. He admitted making mistakes
   B. He corrected "errors in his calculations"
   C. He was truly objective in his judgments
   D. He enjoyed "the most notable triumph"

3. In the words "behold this man!" (line 15), the author expresses   3.____

   A. admiration for Turner
   B. awe at Joyce's ULYSSES
   C. approval of Justice Woolsey's decision
   D. amazement at Turner's shifting opinions

4. According to this passage, the reader could most reasonably conclude that ULYSSES

   A. was not known in the United States for several years after it was published
   B. was universally applauded when it was first published
   C. could not be sold legally in the United States before 1933
   D. was James Joyce's first book

5. Which statement concerning the author's attitude toward the "younger intellectuals" is most nearly correct?

   A. They are too rash.
   B. They are receptive to new ideas.
   C. They are looking to the critics for guidance.
   D. They are disillusioned with the past.

6. The author's statements about Turner are supported by

   A. hints
   B. generalities
   C. quotations
   D. analogies

KEY (CORRECT ANSWERS)

1. C
2. B
3. D
4. C
5. B
6. C

TEST 3

DIRECTIONS: The passage below is followed by 6 incomplete statements or questions about the passage. Each question or incomplete statement is followed by several suggested answers or completions. Select the one that BEST answers the question or completes the statement. *PRINT THE LETTER OF THE CORRECT ANSWER IN THE SPACE AT THE RIGHT.*

    The way novels go these days,
    beginning slowly then sinking
    inexorably into terror,
    frightens me.

5 Our lives, narrated in the first person,
    touched, when we think of it,
    with a bit of irony,
    compose, of course, a story.

    I like our flat beginning,
10 prefer its bleak New York geography
    and subtle shifting feelings
    to manic extremes.

    I know our ending, death
    and resurrection and find it
15 both deserved and undeserved.
    It does not frighten me.

    But the pages between!
    Please, Lord,
    let then not be
20 extreme.

1. The title of this poem suggests that life will contain

   A. death
   B. loss of faith
   C. insanity
   D. suffering

2. In his prayer, the poet asks that he

   A. live a long and happy life
   B. earn eternal life
   C. live free of unusual events
   D. be able to appreciate the contradictions in life

3. Which BEST states the main idea of the second stanza?

   A. The irony in life is unimportant
   B. We each want to tell our own life story.
   C. Every person's life is a narrative.
   D. All people should write a book about their lives.

4. In the third stanza, the poet suggests that the initial stage of life is

   A. sinister
   B. calm
   C. insane
   D. disappointing

5. In the fourth stanza, the poet suggests that

   A. people partially earn their manner of death and its aftermath
   B. the way people think determines their experiences in life
   C. the way people live determines the way they die
   D. good people welcome death and deserve eternal life

6. The poet's attitude about the end of life could BEST be described as

   A. courageous
   B. eager
   C. calm
   D. irrational

KEY (CORRECT ANSWERS)

1. D
2. C
3. C
4. B
5. A
6. C

TEST 4

DIRECTIONS: The passage below is followed by 6 incomplete statements or questions about the passage. Each question or incomplete statement is followed by several suggested answers or completions. Select the one that BEST answers the question or completes the statement. *PRINT THE LETTER OF THE CORRECT ANSWER IN THE SPACE AT THE RIGHT.*

      Many archeologists assume that Ice Age animal images represent only a form of hunting magic. The hunter, so the theory runs, made an animal image and "killed" it, then went out and hunted with the power of magic on his side. Still other archeologists theorize that
5 the animals were totems—figures of ancestor animals from which different human groups or clans supposedly descended. The animals have also been interpreted as sexual symbols, with certain species representing the male principle and others the female. I was now to ask new questions.
10   When I put the Vogelherd horse under the microscope, I discovered that its ear, nose, mouth and eye and been carefully and accurately carved, but that these features had been worn down by long handling. The figure had obviously been kept by its owner and used for a considerable period. Clearly it had not been created for the purpose
15 of being "killed" at once.
      But in the shoulder of the horse was engraved one unworn angle that I took to represent a dart or wound. Apparently some time late in the use of this figure, it *had* been killed. But why? Was the killing intended as hunting magic? Perhaps. But if Cro-Magnon
20 was as sophisticated as I was beginning to find he was, could the killing not have been for some other symbolic purpose, such as initiation, the casting of a spell, the curing of illness, a sacrifice for the coming winter, or the celebration for the coming spring?
      Whatever the meaning, here was an indication that Ice Age images,
25 like notations and certain tools, were made to be kept and used over a long period for specific purposes.

1. In line 5, the dash is used to

   A. take the place of a semicolon
   B. set off a definition
   C. introduce a list
   D. indicate that something has been left out

2. According to this pasaage, figures such as the Vogelherd horse may have been used by Ice Age

   A. individuals as some kind of symbol
   B. tribes as currency
   C. tribes as objects of worship
   D. hunters as trophies for big kills

1.____

2.____

151

3. The author's purpose in examining the Vogelherd horse was to

   A. discover its origin
   B. analyze its construction
   C. question its significance
   D. determine its age

4. What does this passage imply about the author?

   A. He is not familiar with Cro-Magnon man's hunting strategies
   B. He has personally examined numerous Ice Age artifacts
   C. He has found new evidence about Cro-Magnon man from recent diggings
   D. He has known about the significance of the Vogelherd horse for a long time

5. Which sentence BEST summarizes the main idea of this passage?

   A. "Many archeologists assume that Ice Age animal images represent only a form of hunting magic." (lines 1 and 2)
   B. "I was now to ask new questions." (lines 8 and 9)
   C. "Clearly, it had not been created for the purpose of being 'killed' at once." (lines 14 and 15)
   D. "Whatever the meaning, here was an indication that Ice Age images, like notations and certain tools, were made to be kept over a long period for specific purposes." (lines 24 through 26)

6. The overall tone of this passage may be BEST described as

   A. argumentative
   B. questioning
   C. suspenseful
   D. humorous

KEY (CORRECT ANSWERS)

1. B
2. A
3. C
4. B
5. D
6. B

TEST 5

DIRECTIONS: The passage below is followed by 7 incomplete statements or questions about the passage. Each question or incomplete statement is followed by several suggested answers or completions. Select the one that BEST answers the question or completes the statement. *PRINT THE LETTER OF THE CORRECT ANSWER IN THE SPACE AT THE RIGHT.*

    I saw him look that last look away beyond me into a sky so full of light that I could not follow his gaze. The little breeze flowed over me again, and nearby a mountain aspen shook all of its tiny leaves. I suppose I must have had an idea then of what I was going
5 to do, but I never let it come up into consciousness. I just reached over and laid the hawk on the grass.
    He lay there a long minute without hope, unmoving, his eyes still fixed on that blue vault above him. It must have been that he was already so far away in heart that he never felt the release from my
10 hand. He never even stood. He just lay with his breast against the grass.
    In the next second after that long minute he was gone. Like a flicker of light, he had vanished with my eyes full on him, but without actually seeing even a premonitory wing beat. He was gone
15 straight into that towering emptiness of light and crystal that my eyes could scarcely bear to penetrate. For another long moment there was silence. I could not see him. The light was too intense. Then from afar up somewhere a cry came ringing down.
    I was young then and had seen little of the world, but when I
20 heard that cry my heart turned over. It was not the cry of the hawk I had captured; for, by shifting my position against the sun, I was now seeing further up. Straight out of the sun's eye where she must have been soaring restlessly above us for untold hours, hurtled his
25 mate. And from far up, ringing from peak to peak of the summits over us, came a cry of such unutterable and ecstatic joy that it sounds down across the years and tingles among the cups of my quiet breakfast table.

1. In line 1, "that last look" suggests that the hawk

   A. has been blinded
   B. expects to be rescued
   C. believes his death is near
   D. cannot comprehend what is happening

2. In line 5, the clause "I never let it come up into consciousness" suggests that the freeing of the hawk is

   A. premeditated   B. impulsive
   C. impossible   D. accidental

3. In line 5, the pronoun "it" refers to the

   A. narrator's plan of action   B. captured hawk
   C. mate of the hawk   D. act of trapping the hawk

4. In line 7, the minute is "long" to the narrator because he

   A. is thinking of changing his mind
   B. is young and inexperienced
   C. regrets the action he is taking
   D. is not sure what the hawk will do

5. By the end of the passage, the hawk's gaze is probably focused on

   A. the light
   B. mountain peaks
   C. the blue sky
   D. his mate

6. Throughout this passage, the natural phenomenon the narrator seems most impressed by is the

   A. deathlike silence
   B. intense light
   C. steady breeze
   D. blue sky

7. The narrator's most lasting memory is of the

   A. hawk's eyes
   B. bright light
   C. complete stillness
   D. joyous call

KEY (CORRECT ANSWERS)

1. C
2. B
3. A
4. D
5. D
6. B
7. D

TEST 6

DIRECTIONS: The passage below is followed by 7 incomplete statements or questions about the passage. Each question or incomplete statement is followed by several suggested answers or completions. Select the one that BEST answers the question or completes the statement. *PRINT THE LETTER OF THE CORRECT ANSWER IN THE SPACE AT THE RIGHT.*

    The secret of Billy the Kid's greatness as a desperado lay in a marvelous coordination between mind and body. He had not only the will but the skill to kill. Daring, coolness, and quick thinking would not have served unless they had been combined with physical
5 quickness and a markmanship which enabled him to plink a man neatly between the eyes with a bullet, at say, thirty paces. He was not pitted against six-shooter amateurs but against experienced fighters themselves adept in the handling of weapons. The men he killed would have killed him if he had not been their master in a swifter deadli-
10 ness. In times of danger, his mind was not only calm but also singularly clear and nimble, watching like a hawk for an advantage and seizing it with incredible celerity. He was able to translate an impulse into action with the suave rapidity of a flash of light. While certain other men were a fair match for him in target practice,
15 no man in the Southwest, it is said, could equal him in the lightning-like quickness with which he could draw a six-shooter from its holster and with the same movement fire with deadly accuracy. It may be remarked incidentally that shooting at a target is one thing and shooting at a man who happens to be blazing away at you is something entirely
20 different; and Billy the Kid did both kinds of shooting equally well.

1. The main idea of the sentence, "While certain other men... with deadly accuracy," (lines 14 through 17) is that

   A. other men could beat Billy in target practice
   B. Billy did not aim before he fired
   C. Billy could shoot another person faster than anyone else
   D. Billy did most of his shooting in the Southwest

   1.____

2. In line 15, the words "it is said" suggest that the author is basing his conclusion on

   A. oral tradition   B. radio accounts
   C. historical evidence   D. first-hand experience

   2.____

3. Billy the Kid's quickness is compared to that of a

   A. swooping hawk   B. flash of light
   C. speeding bullet   D. blink of an eye

   3.____

4. According to this passage, Billy the Kid's secret of greatness was that he was

   A. an experienced fighter   B. a wonder of coordination
   C. an ideal desperado   D. a good marksman

   4.____

5. The author seems to excuse Billy's murderous ways because Billy

    A. shot men and targets equally well
    B. was so cool and daring
    C. was so quick and accurate
    D. fought only experienced fighters

6. This passage is developed principally by

    A. order of importance   B. relevant details
    C. chronological order   D. definition

7. The tone of this passage is

    A. spiteful   B. satiric
    C. conversational   D. argumentative

KEY (CORRECT ANSWERS)

1. C
2. A
3. B
4. B
5. D
6. B
7. C

TEST 7

DIRECTIONS: The passage below is followed by 7 incomplete statements or questions about the passage. Each question or incomplete statement is followed by several suggested answers or completions. Select the one that BEST answers the question or completes the statement. *PRINT THE LETTER OF THE CORRECT ANSWER IN THE SPACE AT THE RIGHT.*

    Slaight knew the area. It was punishment as punishment should be, and he hated it. But after some fifty hours walking the area, Slaight had come to admire the concept of walking the area. It was time meant to be wasted, good time, weekend time and it was time lost
5 to the cadet punished. Gone. Forever. Slaight derived no small amount of satisfaction from the private notion that he used the area. It was like reading a book, he decided. Only thing was, what you read on the area had to be your own mind.
    Slaight walked along in and out of his small piece of shade, his
10 eyes adjusting and readjusting to the hot late-May sun beating down on the area, turning the fifty-by-hundred-yard rectangle of concrete between the barracks into a stone oven. There were many styles for walking the area. Some guys walked in little informal groups, a few yards apart, as if the company of others afforded quiet solace. Some
15 guys walked slowly, trying to cover as little ground as possible in each three-hour stint on the concrete. Others rushed from one side of the barracks to the other, as if their speed would hurry the clock along. Some guys cruised the area, covering every inch of the hot rectangle, like they were establishing territorial imperative over the
20 ground they walked. Slaight always walked the same strip of ground, down near the gate, loosely following a series of cracks in the concrete which had been patched with tar in a pattern he found...interesting...nonlinear. And so he always walked a slightly crooked path, stepping to the left and right of the tarred cracks, but never on
25 them. Slaight's area style had nothing to do with his politics, which were conservative, and everything to do with his sense of himself, which struggled somewhere in the mucky, ill-defined area inhabited by twenty-one-year-olds.

1. The author suggests that Slaight is using this time to

    A. learn about himself
    B. meet fellow cadets
    C. prepare for class
    D. keep fit through exercise

2. In lines 3 through 5 the statement, "It was time...to the cadet punished," suggests that the cadet most likely

    A. is happy to lose that time
    B. will miss that time
    C. has not used the time well
    D. habitually wastes time

3. The author implies that Slaight is still childish by stating that when Slaight walks the area, he

   A. always walks a crooked path
   B. plays a game of not stepping on cracks
   C. gets dirty with tar
   D. hops from right to left

4. The author implies that if Slaight's area style was the same as his politics, Slaight would most likely

   A. refuse to walk at all
   B. run instead of walk
   C. walk with large groups
   D. walk in a set pattern

5. As used in line 27, the phrase "ill defined area" refers to Slaight's

   A. sense of self
   B. personal satisfaction
   C. walking style
   D. conservative politics

6. The name Slaight, which suggests gray in color, is appropriate for this character because it

   A. suggests his neutral political attitude
   B. resembles the shade he goes in and out of
   C. reinforces his uncertainty about himself
   D. suggests the color of walls

7. An example of the use of irony in this passage is Slaight's

   A. hating the punishment
   B. walking the area
   C. wasting his time
   D. enjoying the walking

KEY (CORRECT ANSWERS)

1. A
2. B
3. B
4. D
5. A
6. C
7. D

TEST 8

DIRECTIONS: The passage below is followed by 7 incomplete statements or questions about the passage. Each question or incomplete statement is followed by several suggested answers or completions. Select the one that BEST answers the question or completes the Statement. *PRINT THE LETTER OF THE CORRECT ANSWER IN THE SPACE AT THE RIGHT.*

We have never regarded the decibel as a particularly trustworthy index of sound. Sound is not easily measured. Some of the loudest sounds wouldn't give a decibel machine the faintest tremor; a hushed voice in a house where someone had died; or a child's
5 finger on the latch of a door where a man is trying to work, timorously testing the lock to see if the man won't come out and play. The quality of sound is much more telling than the volume, and this is true in the city, where noise is inevitable. A country sawmill is rich in decibels, yet the ear adjusts easily to it, and it soon
10 becomes as undisturbing as a cicada on a suburban afternoon. New York's noise, even in its low decibel range, has an irritating quality, full of sharp distemper. It is impatient, masochistic – unlike the noise of Paris, where the shrill popping of high-pitched horns spreads a gaiety and a slightly drunken good nature. Heat
15 has an effect on sound, intensifying it. On a scorching morning, at breakfast in a cafe, one's china coffee cup explodes against its saucer with a fierce report. The great climaxes of sound in New York are achieved in side streets, as in West 44th Street, beneath our window, where occasionally an intestinal stoppage takes place,
20 the entire block laden with undischarged vehicles, the pangs of congestion increasing till every horn is going – a united, delirious scream of hate, every decibel charged with a tiny drop of poison.

1. In lines 2 through 6, the author describes some sounds that are loud not because of their volume but because of their

    A. pitch   B. resonance
    C. vigor   D. context

2. In lines 5 and 6, the child who touches the lock "timorously" does so because the child is

    A. being cautious about disturbing the man
    B. hurrying to go outside
    C. having difficulty with the lock
    D. fussing at being kept waiting

3. As used in line 7, the word "telling" most nearly means

    A. precise   B. significant
    C. disturbing   D. interesting

4. As used in line 17, the word "report" most nearly means

    A. anger   B. shattering
    C. noise   D. violence

5. In lines 19 through 21, the street is described as having a

    A. nervous breakdown
    B. vicious temper
    C. violent headache
    D. digestive blockage

6. Throughout this passage, with which aspect of sound is the author most consistently concerned?

    A. Its quality
    B. Its level
    C. Its importance
    D. Its recurrence

7. The author's main purpose in writing this passage most likely is to

    A. explain the scientific measurement of sound
    B. express judgments about city life
    C. describe sound impressions
    D. evaluate personal reactions

KEY (CORRECT ANSWERS)

1. D
2. A
3. B
4. C
5. D
6. A
7. C

BASIC FUNDAMENTALS OF POETRY

Poetry is usually expressed in verse, though not all verse is poetry, and much of poetic beauty is often found in prose. The diction of poetry is usually more condensed, picturesque, and archaic than that of prose.

The materials of poetry are taken from external nature, from imagination, and from human life.

Blank Verse is that which has no rhyme.

KINDS OF POETRY

Poetry is usually classified as *epic, lyric,* and *dramatic* poetry; sometimes a fourth class is added, - *didactic* poetry. Epic and dramatic poetry are alike in that the essential element of each is a story but in epic poetry the author tells of the acts and words of others, while in dramatic poetry the characters speak and act for themselves.

EPIC POETRY

Epic poetry includes five varieties, as follows:

1. The Great Epic must have a noble subject, serious treatment, a hero, events largely under superhuman control, and a consistent plot. The interest lies in the action. Examples: The ILIAD and the ODYSSEY; PARADISE LOST.

2. The Metrical Romance differs from the great epic in its theme, which is less serious; its meter, which is lighter; and its control of events, which is mainly human; the love element is more prominent in this form of the epic. Examples: Scott's MARMION and THE LADY OF THE LAKE.

3. The Tale is a simple form of narrative poetry telling a complete story. Examples: Chaucer's CANTERBURY TALES: Tennyson's ENOCH ARDEN.

4. The Ballad is a direct, rapid , and condensed story, having peculiarities of phrase and poetic accent. The common ballad meter is iambic tetrameter alternating with iambic trimeter, in stanzas of four lines each. Examples: CHEVY CHASE; Coleridge's ANCIENT MARINER.

5. Pastorals and Idylls have a great deal of de -scription, often of simple country scenes, mingled with the narrative. Examples: Goldsmith's DESERTED VILLAGE; Tennyson's IDYLLS OF THE KING.

DRAMATIC POETRY

Dramatic poetry tells a story by means of characters speaking and acting in such a way as to develop a plot. The drama is divided into acts, often five, the fifth act showing the results of the plot which has been developing.

The classes of dramatic poetry are tragedy and comedy.

Tragedy deals with the grave situations and problems of life and engenders in the spectator noble emotions.

Comedy deals with the pleasanter and more trivial side of life and chooses its subjects from everyday follies, accidents, or humors.

An Opera is a tragedy or a comedy in which the characters sing their parts.

The following are special forms of comedy:

1. The Farce presents ridiculous and exaggerated situations and characters. It is usually short.

2. The Melodrama is a form of comedy employing music to some extent, and using situations that are very romantic and sensational.

3. The Mask is an old form of comedy introducing much of the spectacular, some music, rural scenes, and supernatural characters.

LYRIC POETRY

Lyric poetry expresses the deepest emotions or sentiment of the poet. The lyric, as the word suggests, was originally designed to be sung to the music of the lyre.

Lyric poetry includes five classes, as follows:

1. Song may be either sacred or secular.

2. The Ode is the loftiest form of lyric, and expresses great range and depth of feeling. This range of emotion often varies the meter. Examples: Tennyson's ODE ON THE DEATH OF THE DUKE OF WELLINGTON; Lowell's COMMEMORATION ODE.

3. The Elegy laments the fleeting condition of human affairs. Examples: Gray's ELEGY WRITTEN IN A COUNTRY CHURCHYARD; Milton's LYCIDAS; Tennyson's IN MEMORIAM.

4. The Sonnet is a short poem of fourteen iambic pentameter lines, and had originally a prescribed arrangement of rhyming lines. The great English sonnet writers are Shakespeare, Milton, Wordsworth, and Mrs. Browning.

What is a sonnet? Tis the pearly shell	a
That murmurs of the far-off murmuring sea;	b
A precious jewel carved most curiously;	b
It is a little picture painted well.	a
What is a sonnet? 'Tis the tear that fell	a
From a great poet's hidden ecstasy;	b
A two-edged sword, a star, a song - ah me!	b
Sometimes a heavy-tolling funeral bell.	a
This was the flame that shook with Dante's breath;	a
The solemn organ whereon Milton played,	b
And the clear glass where Shakespeare's shadow falls:	c
A sea this is - beware who ventureth!	a
For like a fiord the narrow floor is laid	b
Mid-ocean deep to the sheer mountain walls.	c

5. Many lyrics have none of the special aims already mentioned. These may be called Simple lyrics. Example: Burns's TO A DAISY.

DIDACTIC POETRY

Didactic verse is not the highest type of poetry. Its aim is primarily to instruct. Example: Pope's ESSAY ON MAN.

Poetry that teaches a moral truth is not necessarily to be classed as didactic verse.

One form of didactic poetry is satirical in its tone, thereby adding sharpness to the truth of the intended teaching. Example: Lowell's BIGLOW PAPERS.

METER

Verse is composition arranged in regularly recurring accents and pauses.

The unit of measure in verse is the Foot. Every foot in poetry (except the spondee, the pyrrhic foot and the tribach) has one accented syllable and one or more unaccented syllables.

Every line of verse has usually at least two pauses. One comes in the body of the line and is called a Caesura, or a caesural pause. The other comes at the end of the line and is called the final pause. Both these pauses must be observed in reading' verse.

Reading verse to show its meter is called Scansion.

Accented syllables may be marked by a macron (-) or by the acute accent (') . Unaccented syllables may be marked by a breve (ᴗ).

POETIC LINES

Monometer	=	line of one foot
Dimeter	=	line of two feet
Trimeter	=	line of three feet
Tetrameter	=	line of four feet
Pentameter	=	line of five feet
Hexameter	=	line of six feet
Heptameter	=	line of seven feet
Octameter	=	line of eight feet

POETIC FEET

A foot of two syllables with the accent on the first is a Trochee, or a Trochaic Foot (- ᴗ).

A foot of two syllables with the accent on the second is an Iambus, or an Iambic Foot (ᴗ -).

A foot of two syllables, both accented, is a Spondee, or a Spondaic Foot (--).

A foot of two syllables, neither accented, is a Pyrrhic Foot (ᴗᴗ) .

A foot of three syllables with the accent on the first syllable is a Dactyl, or a Dactylic Foot (- ᴗᴗ).

A foot of three syllables with the accent on the last syllable is an Anapest, or an Anapestic Foot (ᴗᴗ -).

A foot of three syllables, no one accented, is a Tribrach.

A pyrrhic foot and a tribrach are made up of unimportant words and unaccented syllables.

Some lines show two or more kinds of feet. Such lines are said to be mixed.

A line is named from the prevailing foot.

$$\cup - = \text{iambus}$$
$$-\cup = \text{trochee}$$
$$-- = \text{spondee}$$
$$\cup\cup = \text{pyrrhic foot}$$
$$-\cup\cup = \text{dactyl}$$
$$\cup\cup - = \text{anapestic foot}$$
$$\cup\cup\cup = \text{tribrach}$$

```
 ∪   ∪    ∪     ∪    ∪ -  ∪   -
I wan | dered lone | ly as | a  cloud
```
(Iambic tetrameter)

```
 -  ∪    - ∪    - ∪   - ∪
Hear the | lapping | of the | water
```
(Trochaic tetrameter)

```
 -  ∪ ∪    - ∪ ∪   - ∪  ∪   - ∪ ∪
This is the | forest pri | meval; the | murmuring
```

```
 -  ∪ ∪   -   ∪
pines and the | hemlocks
```
(Dactylic hexameter)

```
 ∪  -     ∪ ∪ -    ∪ ∪  -    ∪ ∪  -
Oh, young | Lochinvar | is come out | of the West
```
(Anapestic tetrameter)

```
 -  ∪  ∪   - ∪ ∪
One more un | fortunate
```
(Dactylic dimeter)

```
 ∪  -    ∪ -    ∪  -   ∪ -   ∪  -
This was | the no | blest Ro | man of | them all
```
(Iambic pentameter)

FIGURES OF SPEECH

Figures of speech are used to make language more effective. The common figures are *metaphor, simile, allegory, personification, apostrophe, metonymy, euphemism, hyperbole, antithesis, irony, climax, onomatopoeia,* and *alliteration.*

Metaphor and Simile are figures based on resemblance; metaphor implies the comparison, while simile expresses it, usually by either *like* or *as.*

Metaphor:

"Hearty and hale was he, an oak that is covered with snowflakes."

Simile:

"Lightsome as a locust leaf,
 Sir Launfal flashed forth in his unscarred mail."

"The gentlemen choristers have evidently been chosen, like old Cremona fiddles, more for tone than looks."

Allegory is a prolonged metaphor used to teach some abstract truth by the use of symbols. Examples: Bunyan's PILGRIM'S PROGRESS; Spenser's FAERIE QUEENE; Psalm lxxx., in which the "vine" stands for the people of Israel.

Personification attributes life to inanimate objects. When the object is directly addressed, the figure is called Apostrophe.

Personification:

"The little brook heard it and built a roof
'Neath which he could house him, winter proof."

Apostrophe:

 "But, O Grief, where hast thou led me!"

Metonomy is the substitution of one name for another which it suggests. Examples:

"She keeps a good table."
"The pen is mightier than the sword."

Euphemism is a softened way of expressing an unpleasant thought.

Direct: He is a liar.
Euphemistic: He is purposely inaccurate in his statements.
Hyperbole is effective exaggeration.

 "her eye in heaven
Would through the airy region stream so bright,
That birds would sing and think it were not night."

"her eye in heaven
Would through the airy region stream so bright,
That birds would sing and think it were not night."

Antithesis is a contrast of words or thoughts. Examples:

"Better be first, he said, in a little Iberian village
Than be second in Rome."

"Fools rush in where angels fear to tread."

Irony is hidden satire.

"'Tis pretty, sure, and very probable,
That eyes, that are the frail'st and softest things,
Should be called tyrants, butchers, murderers."

Climax states a series of thoughts in the order of their importance, the most important last. A reversal of this order is sometimes used for humorous effect and is called Anti-climax.

Examples of Climax:

"It is an outrage to bind a Roman citizen; to scourge him is an atrocious crime; to put him to death is almost parricide; but to crucify him—what shall I call it?"

Onomatopœia emphasizes the meaning of adapting the sound to the sense. Example from CATARACT OF LODORE:

"And sounding and bounding and rounding,
And bubbling and troubling and doubling,
And grumbling and rumbling and tumbling,
And clattering and battering and shattering."

Alliteration repeats the same sound in successive words. Examples:

"Silently out of the room there *g*lided the *g*listening savage,
Bearing the *s*erpent's *s*kin and *s*eeming himself like a *s*erpent,
*W*inding his sinous *w*ay in the *d*ark to the *d*epths of the forest."

CPSIA information can be obtained
at www.ICGtesting.com
Printed in the USA
LVHW021907171219
640814LV00021B/325